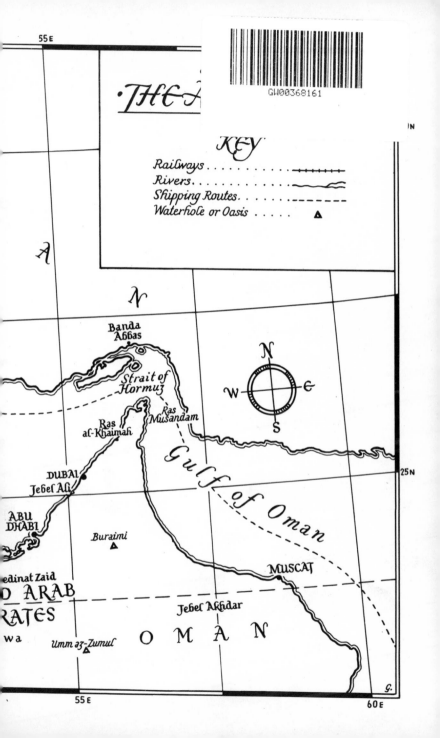

Inshore Fishes of the Arabian Gulf

Inshore Fishes of the Arabian Gulf

Kenneth Relyea

Department of Biology, Jacksonville University, Jacksonville, Florida

with illustrations by ROBERT CHARLES

London
GEORGE ALLEN & UNWIN
Boston   Sydney

First published in Great Britain in 1981

GEORGE ALLEN & UNWIN LTD
40 Museum Street, London WC1A 1LU-

© Kenneth Relyea, 1981

British Library Cataloguing in Publication Data

Relyea, Kenneth
  Inshore fishes of the Arabian Gulf. – (The
  natural history of the Arabian Gulf.)
  1. Marine fishes – Persian Gulf
  I. Title   II. Series
  597'.0927'35   QL622.32   80-41341

  ISBN 0-04-597003-3

Set in 11 on 12 point Times by Western Printing Services Ltd, Bristol
and printed in Great Britain
by Biddles Ltd, Guildford, Surrey

To my students at Kuwait University

Contents

9

Illustrations

PLATES

11

Plate VII
  a. *Pristotis jerdoni*
  b. *Mugil macrolepis*
  c. *Polydactylus sextarius*
  d. *Bathygobius fuscus*
  e. *Boleophthalmus boddarti*

Plate VIII
  a. *Periophthalmus koelreuteri*
  b. *Scartelaos viridis*
  c. *Siganus oramin*
  d. *Synaptura orientalis*

FIGURES

Acknowledgements

I would like to recognise the assistance of Dr Thomas Vaughan, Dr David Clayton, Dr Ian McFarland, Dr John Randall, Dr Bruce Collette, Dr Victor Springer, Dr William Smith-Vaniz, Dr Charles Dawson and Mr John Ferguson for either assistance in the field or help with identifications. Dr Brian Coad provided helpful discussion. Special thanks for encouragement go to Dr John and Anne Cloudsley-Thompson. For help in the field, secretarial assistance, many suggestions and encouragement I am most in debt to my wife, Gail, and our children, John and Lara.

Glossary

Adipose fin	Small fleshy fin not supported by fin rays on the back of some fishes.
Anal fin	The unpaired fin in the ventral midline of the body, behind anus.
Annelid worm	Segmented, marine worm.
Anterior	Towards front.
Axil	Region at the junction of a fin and body.
Axillary process	Enlarged, modified scale at junction of fin and body.
Barbel	Sensory filament, usually on chin or head.
Caniniform	Canine-like teeth; sharp pointed teeth.
Carnivorous	Flesh-eating.
Cartilaginous	With a skeleton composed of cartilage.
Caudal fin	Tail fin.
Caudal peduncle	Portion of body, a stalk, which bears the caudal fin.
Ciguatera	Fish poisoning; toxins accumulated over a long period of time by large predatory fishes from the smaller food items that they eat; dangerous if consumed by humans.
Circumtropical	Throughout tropical areas of the world.
Claspers	Modified portions of the pelvic fins of sharks and rays; used in copulation.
Crustaceans	Crabs, shrimps.
Ctenoid	Rough bony scale typical of many bony fish.
Cycloid	Smooth bony scale typical of many bony fish.
Deciduous	Of scales, for example, which drop off easily.
Demersal	Sinking.
Distal	Away from midline of body.
Dorsal	On or of the back.

15

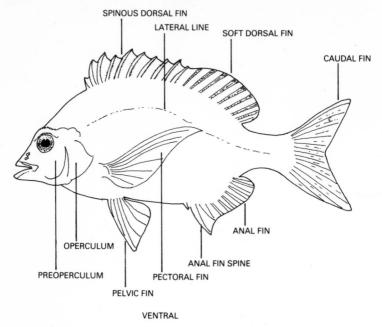

Fig. 1   Generalised Fish Diagram

Elongate	Extended.
Falcate	Sickle-shaped.
Fauna	Animal life.
Finlets	Small, separated fins found posterior to the dorsal fin on some fishes.
Gillrakers	Projections from inner surface of gill arch of fishes; often used to strain plankton in plankton-feeding fishes.
Gill slit(s)	Opening or openings on side of head through which water is expelled.
Herbivorous	Plant-eating.
Hermaphrodite	Both sexes in the same individual.
Incisiform	Incisor-like teeth adapted for biting.
Inter-tidal	Between high and low tide marks.

16

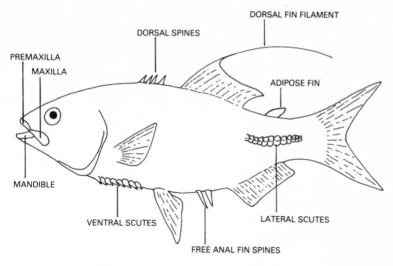

Fig. 2   Generalised Fish Diagram

Invertebrates	Animals without a backbone.
Jugular	In the region of the throat.
Keel	Ridge
Labial fold	Fold of the lips at corner of mouth.
Lateral	At, on or of the sides.
Lunate	Crescent-shaped
Marine	Of the sea.
Maxilla	Upper jaw
Medial	Toward the midline.
Median fins	The unpaired fins; dorsal, anal and caudal fins.
Molariform	Molar-like teeth; flat crushing teeth.
Mollusca	Clams, snails, squids, octopuses.
Ocellus	Dark spot bordered by a lighter-coloured ring.
Omnivorous	Eating both animal and plant material.
Operculum	Covering over gills.
Origin	Beginning.
Oviparous	Egg-laying
Ovoviviparous	Retaining and developing eggs (em-

17

	bryos) in body of female parent; no placenta.
Palate	Roof of mouth.
Pectoral fins	Paired fins anteriorly on sides.
Pelagic	Floating or swimming in the open ocean.
Pelvic fins	Paired fins either on abdomen or in chest region.
Placoid	Type of small scale found on sharks and rays.
Plankton	Small microscopic, or nearly so, floating organisms.
Posterior	Towards tail.
Predorsal	In front of dorsal fin.
Prehensile	Grasping.
Preopercle (or	
Preoperculum)	Bone anterior to operculum bone.
Ray	Soft, flexible fin support; branched at tip.
Scutes	Enlarged scales, usually along the lateral line or in ventral midline of body.
Soft dorsal fin	Also known as second dorsal fin. Fin on back with soft rays as skeletal support.
Spine	Strong unbranched fin support, or a projection from the body or head.
Spinous dorsal fin	Also known as first dorsal fin. Fin on back with strong spine support.
Spiracle	Opening behind eye of rays, guitarfish, skates and relatives (Rajiformes), and some sharks. Used as water intake area in Rajiformes; function unclear in sharks.
Substrate	Layer, for example, of mud or rock.
Sub-terminal	Under the end or tip; projecting downward.
Sutures	Regions where two bones join.
Taxonomy	Science of classifying animals.
Terminal	At the end or tip.
Thoracic	In the region of the chest.
Truncate	Squared, or tending to be squared.

Tubercles	Bumps.
Ventral	On or of the underside.
Viviparous	Retaining and developing embryos in body of female parent; placenta present.
Zooplankton	Small animals floating in ocean; the animal component of plankton.

Geographical Gazetteer

The following list consists of all those localities which are referred to in the text but which do not appear on the map of the Arabian Gulf (see endpapers); the localities marked on the map have not been duplicated on this list.

The map of the Arabian Gulf is reproduced in all volumes of the *Natural History of the Arabian Gulf* series.

Ain al-Abed, Saudi Arabia   28°10′N 48°25′E
Gulf of Salwah, Saudi Arabia/Qatar   25°N 51°E
Jana, Saudi Arabia   27°15′N 50°E
Khor-al-Khafji, Saudi Arabia   28°30′N 48°40′E
Khor-al-Khiran, Kuwait   28°40′N 48°40′E
Kubar, Kuwait   29°N 48°35′E
Mekran, Pakistan   25°N 65°E
Shatt-al-Arab, Iraq/Iran   30°N 48°40′E
Tarut Bay, Saudi Arabia   26°40′N 50°10′E

INTRODUCTION

Existing literature does not provide adequate descriptions and biological information for fishes that might be encountered by people using the shorelines of the Arabian Gulf for recreation, or by scientists new to the area and wanting a useful basic identification guide. In this book I attempt to list the fishes of inshore, shallow waters of the Arabian Gulf, and to provide distinguishing features and biological information for them. As in other works on Arabian Gulf fishes, this is not a complete listing, but it does include families of fishes ignored by others, gives more biological and habitat information where possible, updates the scientific names applied to the species of fishes and, I hope, allows identification of the inshore fishes most commonly encountered along sandy beaches, amongst rock rubble, in tidepools, on coral reefs and grass beds, and even in fish markets. The entire Arabian Gulf is considered, from the Shatt-al-Arab in the north to the Musandam Peninsula and Strait of Hormuz in the south.

This book is designed for use by informed laymen, students and biologists in the Arabian Gulf area. I can only hope that it will be a stepping stone towards greater understanding of the fishes of the Arabian Gulf, and that it will bring enjoyment to its users.

The Arabian Gulf

Bordered by the Arabian Peninsula and Iran, and between 24° and 30° north latitude, the Arabian Gulf is set in an extremely arid region of the world. It is a relatively shallow body of saltwater. Average depth is 35 metres and the deepest areas, along the Iranian coast, are 90–100 metres in depth. The Arabian Gulf is geologically a young basin of

21

saltwater. During the Pleistocene Ice Ages the sea level was markedly lowered, and as little as 18,000–20,000 years ago the Tigris-Euphrates river system extended through what is now the Gulf (Kassler, 1973). Rising sea levels since that time have pushed the Tigris-Euphrates delta northwards to its current position and have established the modern geographical boundaries of the Arabian Gulf. The Gulf is somewhat more than 400 kilometres in length from north-east to south-west, and about 150 km wide in the north and 300 km wide in the south, where it opens into the Gulf of Oman and Indian Ocean through the Strait of Hormuz.

Throughout most of the Arabian Gulf the input of freshwater is exceeded by evaporation. Only in the extreme north, along the coasts of Iran, Iraq, and north-eastern Kuwait, are salinities low, due to the influx of low-salinity water from the Shatt-al-Arab, the only major river outflow to the Arabian Gulf. Rainfall throughout the Gulf area is low and constitutes an insignificant input of freshwater. As a result salinities, measured as the proportion of dissolved salts in the water and expressed as parts per thousand (‰), are usually high, ranging from normal sea water, 35–36‰, to about 40‰ in the open Gulf, and higher in protected coastal embayments. Salinities as high as 70‰ have been recorded from the Gulf of Salwah, Saudi Arabia (Basson et al., 1977).

Coastal water temperatures range from less than 15°C in winter to more than 30°C in summer. The spring and summer seasons may bring dust storms which dump windborne dust into the sea. Much silt is also released from the Shatt-al-Arab estuary.

Shorelines of the Arabian Gulf are a mixture of sand beaches, rock ledges and rock rubble. There is some scattered coral reef development from southern Kuwait southwards through the Gulf, especially around islands such as Kubar in Kuwait and Jana in Saudi Arabia. Mud flats are developed in the north in Kuwait Bay and along the coastlines of Iraq and Iran. Major estuaries exist mainly in the

22

Gulf of Salwah between Saudi Arabia and Qatar, and Tarut Bay, Saudi Arabia. In the north the only indentations in the shoreline, other than Kuwait Bay and the Shatt-al-Arab estuaries, are small inlets at Khor-al-Khiran, Kuwait and Khor al-Khafji, Saudi Arabia. Grass beds occur in shallow water along the coast, and along with the estuaries and inlets constitute major areas of production of marine life.

The fish fauna of the Arabian Gulf

Although rich in number of species, due to a combination of salinity and temperature extremes, siltation from the Shatt-al-Arab and wind-blown dust, and shallowness, the Arabian Gulf contains only a portion of the even richer fauna of the Indian Ocean. Inter-tidal zones may be especially poor in species due to exposure to extreme heat and consequent desiccation, although especially adapted animals such as mudskipper fishes may make use of such habitats where there is soft mud and, by providing flooded burrows, may actually bring about the use of the area by more life forms.

Winter temperatures below critical thresholds (about 20°C) and siltation probably limit coral reef development in the northern Gulf. Where silt is not a problem, especially in the southern Gulf, coral reef development is more extensive and a rich fauna results. The narrowness of the Strait of Hormuz and the impeded flow of water from the Indian Ocean may limit dispersal into the Gulf by Indian Ocean species. The shallowness of the Gulf also limits development of a mid and deep water fauna.

No one knows how many species of fishes exist in the Arabian Gulf; it remains a poorly studied region. Blegvad (1944) made the first extensive survey of fishes along the Iranian coast, and to a lesser extent along the Arabian coast, especially near Bahrain. These were mostly trawl collections, however, and obtained species from somewhat further offshore, as well as inshore. Unfortunately,

23

Blegvad (1944) did not always clearly delineate many species that are closely related and difficult to distinguish. Prior to that work, Regan (1905) provided a list of Arabian Gulf fishes, many of them deep water forms. More recently, White & Barwani (1971) and Kuronuma & Abe (1972) have published descriptions of fishes from the Trucial Coast and Kuwait respectively. Aramco biologists (Basson et al., 1977) have made great progress in characterising habitats in the Arabian Gulf and have provided species lists for both plants and animals, including fishes.

Few fish species appear to be restricted to the Arabian Gulf; most Gulf species exist also in the northern Arabian Sea and Indian Ocean.

How to use this book

Some species of fishes, e.g. anchovies and blennies, to choose two very different types, are often difficult to identify. The reader's attention is therefore called to the generalised fish diagrams, Figs 1 and 2, which show the more important anatomical features used in identification, and to the glossary of terms. Use of descriptions and identification keys are, in part, based on the mastery of these items. I have attempted to find and use the most easily seen or recognised features for the identification of each species. The keys given at various points in the text are a system of opposing choices. You choose the correct statement for the fish you are attempting to identify and go on, as directed, to the next set of opposing choices until you place the specimen in the correct order or family. Identification to species can then be accomplished by referring to the illustrations and descriptions of the species in each family.

Fish are members of the animal Phylum Chordata. Two classes (sub-categories of the Phylum Chordata) of fishes occur in the Arabian Gulf, the Class Chondrichthyes (sharks and rays), and Class Osteichthyes (bony fish). Each class is further sub-divided into more restrictive categories, i.e. order, family, genus and species (the most restrictive category). The scientific name of an animal is formed from the generic (genus) name and specific (species) name. For example, the scientific name of the popular Arabian Gulf food fish, the Hamoor, is *Epinephelus tauvina*. The sequence in which the orders and families of fishes are presented in this book follows that of Nelson (1976).

The distribution in the Arabian Gulf and the overall distribution of each species are noted, followed by its identification characteristics, maximum size, habitat and any other pertinent biological information. Other names by which the species has been, or is, known are given.

Key to the orders of Arabian Gulf fishes

1. a. More than one pair of
      external gill slits   2
   b. Only one pair of external
      gill slits   3
2. a. Gill slits lateral in position   Squaliformes
                                         (sharks)
   b. Gill slits ventral in
      position; body flattened   Rajiformes (rays)
3. a. No spines in the dorsal fin   4
   b. One or more spines in the
      dorsal fin   9
4. a. Both eyes on same side of
      body ....   Pleuronectiformes
                                         (flounders, soles)
   b. Eyes normal in position   5
5. a. Jaws fused to form a
      tubular snout ....   Syngnathiformes
                                         (pipefishes, seahorses)
   b. Jaws not fused to form a
      tubular snout   6
6. a. Adipose fin present ....   Myctophiformes
                                         (lizardfishes)
   b. No adipose fin   7
7. a. No pelvic fins, or pelvic
      fins reduced to a pair of
      stout spines ....   Tetraodontiformes
                                         (puffers, triggerfishes)
   b. Pelvic fins present   8
8. a. Numerous, filamentous
      gill rakers ....   Clupeiformes
                                         (herrings, shads)

b. Gill rakers not numerous
nor filamentous .... Atheriniformes
(silversides, needle-
fishes)

9. a. A single, large spine in the
dorsal fin .... Siluriformes
(catfishes)

b. More than one spine in
the dorsal fin 10

10. a. Three dorsal fin spines;
body without scales;
pelvic fins jugular in
position .... Batrachoidiformes
(toadfishes)

b. More than three dorsal
spines, or three dorsal
spines and body covered
with scales; pelvic fins
usually thoracic in
position 11

11. a. A strong spine (bony
stay) beneath the eye;
head generally spiny or
with hard bony plates .... Scorpaeniformes
(scorpionfishes)

b. No strong spine beneath
eye; head usually without
strong spines, and with
normal scales .... Perciformes
(perch-like fishes)

Class CHONDRICHTHYES

Two categories of fishes are included in this class, the chimaeras or ratfishes (sub-class Holocephali), and the sharks, rays, skates and their relatives (sub-class Elasmobranchii). Only the latter is of importance in the inshore areas of the Arabian Gulf.

Elasmobranch fishes are characterised by a cartilaginous skeleton and small tooth-like scales (called placoid scales or dermal denticles) which give the skin a rough texture. A gill covering, or operculum, is absent in elasmobranchs and from five to seven external pairs of gill slits are therefore visible.

Males have a specialised pair of mating organs, or 'claspers', which are modified portions of the pelvic fins. Fertilisation is internal, and development of the embryos is either internal, or external in a leather encasement, a 'mermaid's purse', which is released by the female and is attached by slender tendrils to rocks or vegetation but is often found washed up on beaches. The release of eggs, in this case a 'mermaid's purse', is termed the oviparous condition (ovi = egg and parous = shedding). Internal development in the uterus of the female is more common in elasmobranchs, however, and two slightly different conditions are known; one in which there is a placental attachment from embryo to mother (the viviparous condition), and one in which the embryo, although retained in the uterus, is nourished by its own yolk sac (the ovoviviparous condition).

Teeth may be sharp, pointed and in many rows (as in most sharks), or flattened plates for crushing molluscs and crustaceans (as in most rays and skates). The mouth of elasmobranchs is usually situated on the underside. The skull of Chondrichthyes is smooth (no sutures) in contrast to that of bony fishes (class Osteichthyes).

Sharks may be placed in from one to several orders, depending on the classification followed. In any case, the sharks (order Squaliformes) can be distinguished from the rays, skates, guitarfishes and sawfishes in that they have gill slits on their sides as opposed to the ventral gill slits of the rays and their relatives (order Rajiformes). The guitar-fishes and sawfishes come somewhere between sharks and rays in the shape of their body and tail, but have ventral gill slits. The rays and skates have a long tapering tail and a wide, flat body. The Rajiformes also have a well developed spiracle (a dorsal opening for water intake) behind the eye: the spiracle is reduced or absent in sharks. All families of Arabian Gulf Chondrichthyes are included in the following key, but only important inshore families are covered in the subsequent text.

Key to the Families of Chondrichthyes in the Arabian Gulf

1. a. Gill slits lateral .... 2 Squaliformes (sharks)

   b. Gill slits ventral. .... 7 Rajiformes (rays, skates etc.)

2. a. Fleshy labial (lip) folds at the angle of the jaw. ...... Orectolobidae (cat or carpet sharks)

   b. No labial folds at jaw angles 3

3. a. Gill openings very large; mouth terminal .... Rhincodontidae (large, plankton-feeding whale sharks; not considered in this book)

30

b. Gill openings normal;
mouth sub-terminal   4

4. a. Head expanded laterally,
like a hammer ....   Sphyrnidae
(hammerhead sharks;
not considered in this
book)

   b. Head not expanded
laterally and not hammer-
like   5

5. a. Fifth gill slit in front of
pectoral fin   6
   b. Fifth gill slit over pectoral
fin ....   Charcharinidae
(requiem sharks)

6. a. Dorsal fins preceded by a
spine ....   Squalidae
(not considered in this
book)

   b. Dorsal fins not preceded
by a spine ....   Lamnidae
(white shark; not
considered in this
book)

7. a. Tail a long tapering
filament   8
   b. Tail not a long tapering
filament   9

8. a. Head distinct from body
disc ....   Myliobatidae
(eagle rays; not
considered in this
book)

   b. Head not distinct from
body disc ....   Dasyatidae
(stingrays)

9. a. Snout prolonged as a saw — Pristidae (sawfishes; not considered in this book)

   b. Snout not prolonged as a saw 10

10. a. Body disc extremely broad; tail very short ..... Gymnuridae (butterfly rays)

    b. Body rounded or elongate; tail not very short 11

11. a. Body disc rounded; snout rounded .... Torpedinidae (electric rays)

    b. Body elongate; snout elongate .... Rhinobatidae (guitarfishes)

Order SQUALIFORMES

Sharks; mostly marine fishes; predators; gill slits on sides of head.

Family ORECTOLOBIDAE

Cat sharks, or carpet sharks, are small, sluggish, harmless sharks found throughout the tropical and sub-tropical Indo-Pacific and Atlantic oceans. They feed on bottom dwelling invertebrates such as molluscs and crustaceans. Oviparous. Eyes are small and there is a spiracle behind each eye. Snout broadly rounded and teeth small. Fleshy labial folds at the jaw angles. One common species in the Arabian Gulf.

Chiloscyllium griseum Müller and Henle

Cat shark (Fig. 3)

Throughout Arabian Gulf; Africa to East Indies.

An inhabitant of shallow waters with sand or sand-mud bottoms. In addition to the family characteristics, the Cat shark may be recognised by the light brown coloration on the back which shades to an even lighter brown on the abdomen. The anal fin is behind the second dorsal fin. Length: 60 cms.

Fig. 3   *Chiloscyllium griseum*

Family CHARCHARINIDAE

The true sharks, the largest family of sharks, are large, active, powerful animals which are all predators and potentially dangerous to man. Ovoviviparous. Teeth large and sharp. The second dorsal fin is directly over the anal fin, and the caudal peduncle lacks a keel. Although six or more species probably occur in the Arabian Gulf, only one is common in inshore areas. The taxonomy of Arabian Gulf sharks is in need of critical study.

Charcharinus menisorrah (Müller and Henle)

Grey reef shark (Fig. 4)

Throughout Arabian Gulf; Red Sea to Japan.

Commonly seen in fish markets. Characterised by a black blotch in the second dorsal fin. Potentially dangerous to humans. Length: 2 m.

Fig. 4   *Charcharinus menisorrah*

Charcharinus spallanzani (LeSeur)   Black-tip shark
Throughout Arabian Gulf; Indian Ocean.

Black-tip sharks are apparently common in the southern Arabian Gulf, especially on coral reefs. Fins are black-tipped. Length: 3 m.

Other species
Charcharinus lamia (Blainville), also known as *C. gangeti-cus* (Müller and Henle), has been found in the Shatt-al-Arab in the north and surely occurs throughout the Arabian Gulf and Indian Ocean. This species attains a length of about 2·5 m and is considered dangerous. Two other species, *C. sorrah* (Müller and Henle) and *C. limba-tus* (Müller and Henle) have been recorded from the Gulf, but are apparently rare.

Order **RAJIFORMES**

Rays, skates, guitarfishes, sawfishes; mostly marine, often estuarine, predators; gill slits ventral in position and a large spiracle present behind each eye.

Family RHINOBATIDAE

Guitarfishes are sluggish, bottom-dwelling rays of the Atlantic and Indo-Pacific seas. Common in shallow water, especially in brackish estuaries and bays. Feed on bottom-dwelling crustaceans, molluscs and other invertebrates. These fish are reputedly good to eat. Ovoviviparous. Body elongate as in sharks, but gill slits open ventrally. The body is flattened so that the eyes are positioned on the top of the head. Pectoral fins are fused to the head, teeth are small, and there is a large spiracle opening behind each eye. The tail is thicker than in other rays and there is no stinging spine. Three common species in the Arabian Gulf.

Rhina ancylostoma Schneider   Short-nosed mud-skate
Throughout Arabian Gulf; Africa to Arabian Sea.
   A bizarre, round-snouted guitarfish with strong tubercles on the head and shoulders. The body may have white spots. Length: 3 m.

Rhinobatos granulatus Cuvier and Valenciennes
                          Granulated guitarfish (Plate I)
Throughout Arabian Gulf; Indian Ocean.
   A common, grey-coloured guitarfish commonly seen in fish markets. Most common in the northern Gulf and enters the Shatt-al-Arab. Snout pointed. No white spots on body. Length: 1 m.

Rhynchobatus djiddensis (Forskål)

White-spotted guitarfish (Plate I)

Throughout Arabian Gulf; Red Sea to Japan.

A common inhabitant of shallow sand or sand-mud substrates, this guitarfish is easily recognised by its white spots.
There is usually a large, dark, white-bordered spot (an
ocellus) at the base of each pectoral fin, in the shoulder
region. Snout pointed. This species is said to be very good
to eat. Length: 3 m.

Other species
Rhinobatos annulatus Müller and Henle has been reported
from the Arabian Gulf, but this should be verified with
additional specimens.

Family TORPEDINIDAE

Torpedo rays, or numbfish, are bottom-dwelling species of
the Indo-Pacific and Atlantic oceans. They are usually
found buried in sand bottoms in shallow water. Paired
electric organs behind the large spiracles can deliver a
dangerous electric shock. Feed on molluscs and crustaceans. Ovoviviparous. The body disc is nearly round, the
caudal fin is truncate, and the two dorsal fins are situated
over the pelvic fins. Three species are known from the
Arabian Gulf.

Narcine timlei (Bloch and Schneider)   torpedo ray
Known from northern Arabian Gulf; Indian Ocean.

Probably rare in the Gulf. First dorsal fin entirely behind
pelvic fins. Length: 30 cms.

Torpedo marmorata Risso   torpedo ray (Fig. 5)
= *Torpedo panthera* Olfers

Throughout Arabian Gulf; Africa to Arabian Sea.

This is the most common torpedo ray in the Arabian
Gulf, and can be recognised by its brown-white mottled
colour pattern. Length: 60 cms.

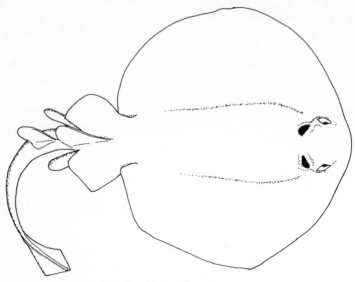

Fig. 5   *Torpedo marmorata*

Torpedo sinus-persici Olfers   torpedo ray
Throughout Arabian Gulf; Red Sea to Arabian Sea.
    Most likely to be encountered in the southern Gulf.
Large dark blotches on body. Length: 15 cms.

Family DASYATIDAE

Stingrays are a worldwide family of bottom-dwelling fishes
of shallow coastal waters and estuaries. Foods consist of
small crustaceans, molluscs, annelid worms and fishes. Not
good to eat as the meat is bitter. Ovoviviparous. The body
is a flattened disc and the pectoral fins are fused to the
head. Gill slits are ventral. The tail is whip-like and bears
one or more spines near the base. Stingrays can inflict a
dangerous wound with these sharp spines. Dorsal and anal
fins are absent. There are three common stingray species in
the Arabian Gulf.

Dasyatis sephen (Forskål)   Fantail stingray
Throughout Arabian Gulf; Africa to Australia and
through much of Pacific Ocean.

A common ray distinguished by a dark grey to brown
body and a very long tail (2–3 times body-disc length).
There is an elevated ridge of skin (a dermal fold) on the
underside of the tail. The body is smooth, but there may be
small tubercles on older individuals. Disc width: 1·5 m.

Himantura gerrardi (Gray)   Gerrard's stingray
Throughout Arabian Gulf; Red Sea to Indian Ocean.

Common in the Gulf, but perhaps more often in deeper
water than other stingrays. The most distinctive feature is

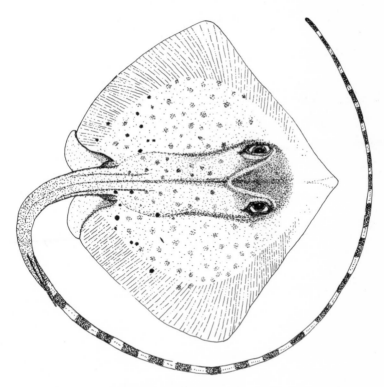

Fig. 6   *Himantura uarnak*

39

the very long tail, 3·5 times the body disc length. Body colour is usually brown with light spots. Disc width: 1·3 m.

Himantura uarnak (Forskål)   Long-tailed ray (Fig. 6)
Throughout Arabian Gulf; Africa to East Indies, Australia.
   A very common stingray distinguished by a pointed snout and the lack of a dermal fold, or ridge, on the tail. The tail is 2–3 times the body disc length. Colour is brown with small dark spots, which may fade with age. Disc width: 1·3 m.

Family GYMNURIDAE

The butterfly rays constitute a wide-ranging family of fishes in shallow seas. They are usually found along coastlines on sandy bottoms, but further from shore than other fishes considered in this book. Feed on bottom-dwelling invertebrates. Ovoviviparous. Body disc much wider than it is long, tail very short, either with or without a spine. One Arabian Gulf species.

Gymnura poecilura (Shaw)   Spotted butterfly ray
Throughout Arabian Gulf; Red Sea to China.
   A common, but little studied species. Length: 50 cms.

Class OSTEICHTHYES

Most fish are members of this class. As the name implies, these fish are characterised by a skeleton of bone, as opposed to cartilage. The skull is sutured, not smooth as in the Chondrichthyes. A bony operculum covers the gills, leaving only one pair of external gill slits. Fins usually have bony supports, either stout, unbranched spines, or softer, branched rays. There is usually no spiracle opening behind the eye. The body is covered either with cycloid (smooth) scales, ctenoid (rough) scales, or is naked. An internal swim, or air, bladder is often present, and externally there is a sensory system of canals and pores known as a lateral line system.

Bony fish are diverse. They occupy fresh and salt water, shallow and deep areas, and a multitude of more specific habitats. The many body forms and colour patterns reflect adaptations to these various situations. Most species are oviparous and the eggs are fertilised externally in the sea water.

Essentially, the bony fish can be divided into two categories, the Sarcopterygii (lungfish and relatives) and Actinopterygii, or Neopterygii, which includes most fish species, and all bony fish in the Arabian Gulf.

Order **CLUPEIFORMES**

Small marine or freshwater fishes; usually plankton-feeders; a single dorsal fin with no spines; long gillrakers; cycloid scales.

Key to the Families of Clupeiformes in the Arabian Gulf

1. a. Large teeth present .... Chirocentridae
                                  (wolf herrings)
   b. Teeth small or absent 2
2. a. Tip of snout extended,
      overhangs mouth .... Engraulidae
                                  (anchovies)
   b. Snout does not overhang
      mouth .... Clupeidae
                                  (herrings, sardines)

Family CLUPEIDAE

Herrings, shads, sardines and relatives are a large group of temperate and tropical fishes. Schooling, zooplankton-feeding fishes, clupeids are in turn eaten by other fishes, birds and humans, and are thus an important part of the oceanic food web. Eggs are either pelagic, or deposited on the sea floor. Some species spawn in freshwater rivers (i.e. Shatt-al-Arab). Characterised by smooth, deciduous scales, a single dorsal fin which lacks spines, forked tail, numerous filamentous gillrakers and no lateral line. Silvery colour. This is a difficult and, to some extent, poorly known group of fishes of the Arabian Gulf. Identification of species is often difficult. The most common inshore species are discussed below, but perhaps fifteen or more species occur in the Gulf.

Dorosoma nasus (Bloch)   Gizzard shad
Throughout Arabian Gulf; Arabia to East Indies.

Commonly enters estuaries. Characterised by elongated last ray of dorsal fin. Length: 20 cms.

Dussumieria acuta Cuvier and Valenciennes
                                          Round herring
Throughout Arabian Gulf; Central Indo-Pacific.

Lacks scutes on the ventral midline of abdomen. Length: 20 cms.

Hilsa ilisha (Hamilton-Buchanan)   River shad
Throughout Arabian Gulf; Red Sea to Indian Ocean.

A common Arabian Gulf species which often enters fresh and brackish water. Characterised by an elongate maxillary bone (upper jaw) which reaches back to the posterior edge of the eye. There are 15–17 scutes in the ventral midline before the pelvic fins, and 14–15 scutes behind the pelvic fins. Length: 50 cms. (Another Arabian Gulf species of this genus is *H. kanagurta*, a deeper bodied and apparently uncommon species.)

Ilisha elongata (Bennett)   Slender shad
Throughout Arabian Gulf; Arabian Sea and Indian Ocean.

A very common species along beaches. Similar to the following species but distinguished from it by the large number of ventral scutes (20–28) in front of the pelvic fins, and small number (8–11) behind the pelvic fins. Length: 40 cms.

Ilisha indica (Swainson)   Indian shad (Fig. 7)
Throughout Arabian Gulf; Arabian Sea, Indian Ocean.

A common species of shad with a rounded (convex) ventral profile and straight dorsal profile. The maxilla is long as in *Hilsa*, but this species may be distinguished from *Hilsa* and *I. elongata* by the number of scutes in front of the

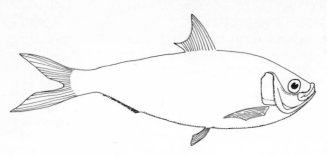

Fig. 7   *Ilisha indica*

pelvic fins (17–20) and behind the pelvic fins (11–14). Length: 40 cms.

Sardinella fimbriata (Cuvier and Valenciennes)   sardine
Throughout Arabian Gulf; Indian Ocean.

The sardines most commonly encountered in the Arabian Gulf are probably this species and the one that follows. *Sardinella fimbriata* is deeper bodied than *S. perforata* and has more gillrakers (65 or more). Length: 15 cms.

Sardinella perforata (Cantor)   sardine
Throughout Arabian Gulf; Arabian Gulf to Philippines.

A very common species which is difficult to distinguish from the preceding, but is more slender and has fewer gillrakers (less than 65). Length: 15 cms.

Family ENGRAULIDAE

Anchovies are small, plankton-feeding fishes of all seas. Some species may enter freshwater. Edible. Produce pelagic eggs. Characterised by a large sub-terminal mouth. The snout markedly overhangs the mouth and the upper jaw extends back to well behind the eye. Jaws are weak. The body may be nearly transparent, and there is often a silvery stripe on the sides. Scales are smooth. There are about six common species in the Arabian Gulf.

Stolephorus heterolobus Rüppell   anchovy
Southern Arabian Gulf; Indo-Pacific.

This species can be identified by a well-defined silver stripe on the sides. In addition, the upper jawbone (maxilla) is rounded at the back, and reaches to the rear edge of the preoperculum bone. Length: 8 cms.

Stolephorus indicus Van Hasselt   anchovy
Throughout Arabian Gulf; wide-ranging in the Indo-Pacific.

Silvery stripe not so well defined as in *S. heterolobus*. Jawbone reaches to front edge of the preoperculum. Length: 10 cms.

Stolephorus zollingeri (Bleeker)   anchovy
= *Stolephorus buccaneeri* Strasburg

Throughout Arabian Gulf; Red Sea to East Indies, Australia.

Not a well-known species. Distinguished from *S. indicus* in that the front (origin) of the anal fin is behind the front of the dorsal fin, not directly below it, and from *S. heterolobus* by the truncate rather than rounded rear edge of the upper jaw. Length: 10 cms.

Thryssa hamiltoni (Gray)   anchovy
= *Engraulis vitirostris* Blegvad and *Scutengraulis hamiltoni* (Gray)

Known only from Iraq, but probably more widespread in the Arabian Gulf; Indo-Pacific.

Upper jaw very long, reaching to the base of the pectoral fin. Length: 14 cms.

Thryssa mystax (Bloch and Schneider)   anchovy
Known from Kuwait, but probably more widespread in the Arabian Gulf; Indian Ocean.

Anal fin origin directly below origin of dorsal fin. Upper jaw extends past operculum, but not quite to the base of the pectoral fin. Length: 20 cms.

Thryssa setirostris (Broussonet)   anchovy
= *Thrissocles setirostris* (Broussonet) and *Clupea seti-rostris* Broussonet
  Known from one specimen from Iraq; Indo-Pacific. Probably more abundant and widespread.
  Identification of this and other Gulf anchovies should be verified. Upper jaw very long, reaching to pelvic fins. Length: 10 cms.

Family CHIROCENTRIDAE

Wolf herrings are found throughout the tropical and sub-tropical Indo-Pacific region. Voracious predators. Considered good to eat, but bony. Elongate, silvery fish with small scales and large canine teeth. Probably only one Arabian Gulf species.

Chirocentrus dorab (Forskål)   Wolf herring (Plate I)
Throughout Arabian Gulf; East Africa to Japan.
  Little is known of the habits of the Wolf herring. Eggs are pelagic. Anal fin much longer than the dorsal fin. Length: 3·5 m.

Order **SILURIFORMES**

Mostly freshwater fishes, a few marine. Stout spine in dorsal and pectoral fins. Scales often absent. Barbels present on chin, at jaw angles, and sometimes in association with the nostrils.

Key to the Families of Siluriformes in the Arabian Gulf

1. a. Adipose fin present ....   Ariidae
   b. No adipose fin ....   Plotosidae
                                       (striped catfish-eel)

Family ARIIDAE

Sea catfishes are marine species which frequently enter brackish estuaries throughout the tropical and sub-tropical seas. These inhabitants of sandy and mud bottoms are nocturnal scavengers. Although edible, they are not popular as food items. Eggs are incubated in the mouth cavity by male fish. About thirty eggs are incubated at one time, and the young are retained for several weeks after hatching. The dorsal fin bears a stout spine and is followed by a fleshy adipose fin. The caudal fin is deeply forked, there are three pairs of barbels (no nasal barbels), and no scales. The dorsal and pectoral fin spines can inflict a painful sting. One species in the Arabian Gulf.

Arius thalassinus (Rüppell)   sea catfish (Fig. 8)
= *Tachysurus thalassinus* (Rüppell)
    Throughout Arabian Gulf; Indo-Pacific.
    This large sea catfish prefers sand and mud bottoms. Dorsal coloration is red-brown; the abdomen is lighter-coloured. *Arius dussumieri* is a name that has been applied

47

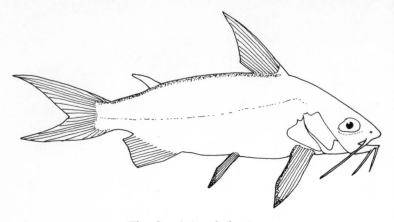

Fig. 8   *Arius thalassinus*

to specimens from the southern Arabian Gulf, but these are probably *A. thalassinus*. Length: 1 m.

Family PLOTOSIDAE

Catfish-eels occur in marine, brackish and fresh water throughout the Indo-Pacific region. Predators. Considered to be edible. Reproductive habits unknown. Slender, scaleless, eel-like catfish with four pairs of barbels. The second dorsal fin and anal fin are continuous with the caudal fin. There is no adipose fin, and the first dorsal fin and pectoral fins bear a stout, sharp spine which can be used to inject a venom. These fish should be regarded as dangerous and care should be taken when handling. One species in the Arabian Gulf.

Plotosus anguillaris (Bloch)   Striped catfish-eel (Fig. 9)
Throughout Arabian Gulf; Africa to Australia, Polynesia, Japan.
    This is a common fish in shallow water in the Arabian Gulf. It occurs in estuaries, along rocky beaches and on coral reefs. Younger individuals can be seen in schools

Fig. 9   *Plotosus anguillaris*

close to shorelines and on coral reefs. Older individuals are more solitary. The body is brown with cream-coloured horizontal stripes. Said to reach a length of 90 cms, but perhaps only half that in the Arabian Gulf.

Order **MYCTOPHIFORMES**

Marine, often deep-sea fishes. No spines in fins. Adipose fin present. Tail forked. One inshore family in the Arabian Gulf.

Family SYNODONTIDAE

Lizardfishes are found in all seas. They are bottom-dwelling predators which burrow into sand. Edible, and commonly seen in fish markets. Large mouth, body scaled, and a straight, conspicuous lateral line. One dorsal fin, but a small adipose fin is also present. Mottled colour patterns provide camouflage. Three species in the Arabian Gulf.

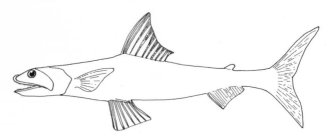

Fig. 10 *Saurida tumbil*

Saurida tumbil (Bloch)   lizardfish (Fig. 10)
Throughout Arabian Gulf; Indo-Pacific.
   Occurs on sand substrates. Can be distinguished from the similar *S. undosquamis* in that it lacks spots on the caudal fin. Known to produce pelagic eggs which float in the ocean currents. Length: 40 cms.

Saurida undosquamis (Richardson) Spotted lizardfish
Throughout Arabian Gulf; Africa to East Indies, Australia, Japan.

Found on sandy substrates. Distinguished by spots along lateral line and on upper portion of tail. Length: 40 cms.

Trachinocephalus myops (Bloch and Schneider)
lizardfish
Known from Kuwait and the UAE, but probably occurs throughout the Arabian Gulf; world-wide distribution in tropics and sub-tropics.

Found in deeper water than *Saurida*. Distinct dark blotch in the shoulder region, and two blue stripes on each side. Length: 30 cms.

Order **BATRACHOIDIFORMES**

Marine, occasionally freshwater. Two dorsal fins, the first small. Pelvic fins anterior to pectoral fins. Usually no scales. Head and mouth large. One inshore family in the Arabian Gulf.

Family BATRACHOIDIDAE

Toadfishes are bottom-dwelling marine and brackish water fishes found in all tropical and sub-tropical seas. Carnivorous. Eggs are placed in a nest of debris or in a crevice and guarded. No scales, or very small, smooth scales, on body. Head large and mouth wide with strong teeth. Two dorsal fins, the first with three stout spines. Spine on the operculum. Coloration brown. One. species in the Arabian Gulf.

Batrachus grunniens (Linnaeus)   Toadfish (Fig. 11)
Throughout Arabian Gulf; Indian Ocean.
    Very common in rocky areas, especially eroded rock rubble and tide pools. The Toadfish hides in crevices and holes by day and is an active predator at night. Eat crabs, shrimp, fish and snails. Eggs are laid in crevices, holes in rocks and possibly in sponge cavities. Length: 20 cms.

Fig. 11 *Batrachus grunniens*

52

Order **ATHERINIFORMES**

Marine and freshwater. One or two dorsal fins, usually one with soft rays. No spines in other fins. Dorsal and anal fins far back on body. Smooth, cycloid scales. Gillrakers short and numerous.

Key to the Families of Atheriniformes in the Arabian Gulf

1. a. Upper and lower jaws prolonged, toothy .... Belonidae (needlefishes)

   b. Upper and lower jaws not prolonged and toothy 2

2. a. Only lower jaw prolonged Hemirhamphidae (halfbeaks)

   b. Neither jaw prolonged ... 3

3. a. First dorsal fin with spines and second dorsal fin with soft rays; first dorsal may be very small; tail forked Atherinidae (silversides)

   b. Soft dorsal fin only; tail not forked, but rounded or square .... Cyprinodontidae (killifishes)

Family HEMIRHAMPHIDAE

Halfbeaks are relatives of the flying fishes and are found throughout the oceans of the world, but especially in the tropics and sub-tropics. Most species are marine, but some are found in freshwater. They are herbivores which eat floating vegetation. Edible. Eggs are attached to floating vegetation by sticky threads. Halfbeaks are unique and easy to recognise because the lower jaw is prolonged and much longer than the upper jaw. The pectoral fins are high on the body and the lower portion of the tail is often prolonged (as a rudder). At least five species occur in the Arabian Gulf.

Hemirhamphus far (Forskål)   Black-barred halfbeak
Known from Saudi Arabia, but this record must be regarded as tentative; Africa to East Indies, Australia.
   Characterised by 4–6 prominent vertical bars on body. Length: 25 cms.

Hemirhamphus georgii (Cuvier and Valenciennes)
                                    halfbeak
= *Rhynchorhamphus georgii* (Cuvier and Valenciennes)
   Throughout Arabian Gulf; Arabia to China.
   Found in inlets, along beaches, and offshore. Triangular part of upper jaw has no scales and is longer than it is broad. Length: 30 cms.

Hemirhamphus marginatus (Forskål)
                              White-banded halfbeak
Throughout Arabian Gulf; Africa to Japan.
   Very common in estuaries, inlets, and close to shorelines. Triangular part of upper jaw is without scales and is broader than it is long. Ten anal rays. Length: 45 cms.

Hyporhamphus limbatus (Cuvier and Valenciennes)
                                    halfbeak
Throughout Arabian Gulf; Arabia to Philippines, China.
   Commonly enters estuaries. Triangular part of upper jaw is scaled and broader than it is long. Fourteen anal rays. Similar to *Hyporhamphus sindensis* in size and appearance, but may be distinguished from that species by the longer lower jaw. In *Hy. limbatus* the extended portion

of the lower jaw is longer than the head length (measured from the posterior edge of the operculum to the tip of the upper jaw), while in *Hy. sindensis* the lower jaw is shorter than or equal to the head length. The name *Hemirhamphus gaimardi* (Cuvier and Valenciennes) has probably been applied to *Hy. limbatus* in the Arabian Gulf. Length: 20 cms.

Hyporhamphus sindensis (Regan)   halfbeak (Plate I)
Throughout Arabian Gulf; Arabian Gulf and Arabian Sea.
   This small halfbeak resembles *Hy. limbatus* (distinguishing features given with description of that species – see above). A common inshore species likely to be encountered in inlets. Length: 15 cms.

Family BELONIDAE

Needlefishes are mostly marine, but sometimes freshwater, fishes found throughout temperate and tropical seas. All species are predators on small fishes. Edible, but bony. Little is known of their reproductive activities, but eggs are attached to floating vegetation. Characterised by extended upper and lower jaws, both of which bear needlelike teeth. Cream or olive in colour with a silver stripe on sides. Three common species in the Arabian Gulf.

Ablennes hians (Cuvier and Valenciennes)
                                    Barred needlefish
Throughout Arabian Gulf; world-wide distribution in tropics.
   A more offshore species than the other needlefishes in the Gulf. Characterised by 6–16 vertical bars on the body. Length: 1 m.

Tylosurus leiurus (Bleeker)   Banded needlefish (Fig. 12)
Throughout Arabian Gulf; Africa to East Indies, Australia.
   Common in inshore areas. Distinguished from *T.*

Fig. 12 *Tylosurus leiurus*

strongylurus by the greater number of anal fin rays (21–23; 13–15 in *T. strongylurus*), and the truncate tail (more rounded in *T. strongylurus*). Length: 1 m.

Tylosurus strongylurus (Van Hasselt)
Black-spot needlefish
Throughout Arabian Gulf; Arabian Gulf to Philippines, Australia.

In addition to the distinguishing characteristics given under the description of *T. leiurus* (see above), this species has a distinctive dark spot at the base of the caudal fin. Length: 50 cms.

Family CYPRINODONTIDAE

Killifishes are found world-wide in marine and fresh water in both the temperate and tropical zones. These are omnivorous fishes. All are egg layers. Characterised by a small, obliquely positioned mouth, smooth scales, rounded or truncate tail, and no spines in the fins. One species is known from the Arabian Gulf, but others occur in interior waters of Iraq and Iran.

Aphanius dispar (Rüppell)   Arabian killifish (Plate II)
Scattered localities in the Arabian Gulf, notably Shatt-al-Arab of Iraq, Kuwait Bay, Khor al-Khiran in Kuwait, the interior oasis of Ain al-Abed in Saudi Arabia, Bahrain; eastern Mediterranean, Red Sea, Arabian Peninsula, Arabian Gulf.

This is a fish of estuaries, inlets, and creeks, but not of exposed sandy shorelines nor of rocky habitats. Omnivorous, but shows a preference for filamentous algae as a food. Males and females differ markedly in coloration (see Plate II). Length: 7 cms.

Family ATHERINIDAE

Silversides occur in marine, brackish, and fresh waters in both tropical and temperate areas. Zooplankton-feeders which form schools in shallow coastal waters or around coral reefs. Produce sticky eggs which adhere to objects in the water. Silversides are characterised by two dorsal fins, but the first, a spinous fin, may be very small and inconspicuous. The caudal fin is forked, pectoral fins are high on the sides, and pelvic fins are positioned forward of the beginning of the dorsal fin, or directly below it. The mouth, moderate in size, is terminal in position. There is a silver stripe on the sides. One species in the Arabian Gulf.

Allanetta forskåli (Rüppell)   Silverside (Plate II)
Throughout Arabian Gulf; Arabian Gulf to Philippines.
  Forms large schools along sandy beaches and in inlets in the Arabian Gulf, and is caught in small seines and cast nets. In addition to the characteristics given for the family Atherinidae, this species can be distinguished, in adult stages, by the darkened tail fin, black tips on the pectoral fins, and black snout. Length: 12 cms.

Order **SYNGNATHIFORMES**

Marine, some freshwater species. Jaws fused to form tubular snout. Scales may be fused to form bony ring-like plates around body. Pelvic fins usually absent.

Family CENTRISCIDAE

Shrimpfishes, or razorfishes, are highly modified fishes found throughout the Indo-Pacific region. They are compressed laterally and possess scales which are fused into plates and which give the appearance of a shrimp-like shell. The midline of the abdomen is a sharp ridge (razor). The head is extended into a tubular snout. A sharp, pointed spine at the posterior tip of the body is actually a modified spine of the dorsal fin; the remainder of the dorsal fin, and the caudal fin, are underneath the spine. Shrimpfishes are nearly transparent. One species in the Arabian Gulf.

Centriscus scutatus Linnaeus   Shrimpfish (Plate II)
Throughout Arabian Gulf; Red Sea to East Indies, China.
   Shrimpfish are often found with snout pointed downward amongst the spines of sea urchins, and on coral reefs. Length: 15 cms.

Family SYNGNATHIDAE

Seahorses and pipefishes are found throughout the oceans of the world. Most species are marine. Food consists of small invertebrates. In all species the female attaches the eggs to the abdomen or tail of the male; in most, the eggs are actually enclosed in a pouch on the male's abdomen. Coloration is usually brown. Jaws are fused and extended to form a tubular mouth. The scales form a series of bony

58

Fig. 13 *Hippocampus kuda*

rings around the body, pelvic fins are absent, and the tail
may be straight (pipefish) or curled and prehensile, or
grasping (seahorses). Syngnathids in the Arabian Gulf are
poorly known, and the number of species is uncertain.

Hippocampus kuda Bleeker   Spotted seahorse (Fig. 13)
Throughout Arabian Gulf; East Africa to Hawaii.
    Often found on coral reefs. Length: 30 cms.

Syngnathus analaricens Duncker   pipefish
Known from Kuwait, but probably occurs throughout the
Gulf; Arabian Sea.
    Pipefishes of the Arabian Gulf are not well-known taxo-
nomically or ecologically. This species appears to be one of
the more common species in inshore waters, and should be
looked for in floating masses of sea weeds such as *Sargas-
sum*. Length: 7 cms.

Order **SCORPAENIFORMES**

Marine. Bony spine, or stay, beneath eye and across cheek to preoperculum. Head generally spiny and with bony plates.

Key to the Familes of Scorpaeniformes in the Arabian Gulf

1. a. First and second dorsal
        fins clearly separate ......   Platycephalidae
                                         (flatheads)

    b. First and second dorsal
        fins connected   2

2. a. Dorsal fin spines long;
        scales usually present ....   Scorpaenidae
                                         (scorpionfish)

    b. Dorsal fin spines short;
        scales usually absent ......   Synancejidae
                                         (stonefish)

Family SCORPAENIDAE

Scorpionfishes and lionfishes are found in all temperate and tropical seas. These are fish of rocky areas and coral reefs. All are carnivores. Arabian Gulf species probably produce floating, pelagic eggs, but ovoviviparity is known to occur in this family. Tropical Indo-Pacific species are often brightly coloured. There is a characteristic bony ridge (called a stay) across the cheek to the preoperculum. The head is generally armed with spines and bony plates. Dorsal spines are long, sharp and pointed, and can inject a toxic venom. These are potentially very dangerous fish. There are about three common inshore species in the Arabian Gulf.

60

Apistus carinatus (Bloch and Schneider)

Black-fin scorpionfish

= *Hypodytes carinatus* (Bloch and Schneider)

Throughout Arabian Gulf; Africa to Japan.

May be found in shallow rocky areas near beaches and inlets. Pectoral fins are entirely black. Length: 20 cms.

Pterois russelli Bennett   Russell's scorpionfish

= *Pterois lunulata* Schlegel

Throughout Arabian Gulf; Africa to Australia, Japan.

Similar to *Pterois volitans*, but probably less common than that species in inshore areas of the Gulf. Distinguished from *P. volitans* by the reduced size of the tentacles above each eye (or tentacles may be lacking). A dangerous species. Length: 30 cms.

Pterois volitans (Linnaeus)   Red fire-fish, or Lionfish

Throughout Arabian Gulf, but most common in the south; Africa to Hawaii.

This is a dangerous species which frequents coral reefs. Distinguished by the long tentacles above each eye and by its red coloration with white-edged black stripes. Length: 35 cms.

Family SYNANCEJIDAE

The highly venemous stonefishes are found throughout the Indo-Pacific region and are predators on fish and invertebrates. Characterised by a large mouth and head, scaleless bodies, and generally grotesque appearance. Venom glands occur at the base of the short dorsal spines and contain potentially lethal toxins. Four inshore species occur in the Arabian Gulf.

Choridactylum multibarbis Richardson

Orange-banded goblinfish

Known from near Bahrain, but probably more widely distributed; Africa to China.

Little is known of this species; it may be uncommon. Body with 2–3 vertical orange bands. Length: 25 cms.

61

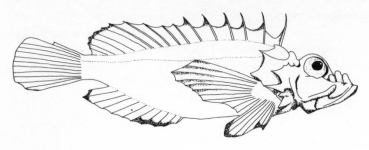

Fig. 14 *Minous monodactylus*

Minous monodactylus (Bloch and Schneider)
Grey goblinfish (Fig. 14)
Throughout Arabian Gulf; Arabian Gulf to China.

This uncommon and more offshore species of stonefish is likely to be encountered only rarely. The dorsal spines appear to be separate because they are connected only toward their bases by a membrane. Length: 12 cms.

Pseudosynanceia melanostigma (Day)
Black-mouth stonefish (Plate III)
Throughout Arabian Gulf; Indian Ocean.

A common stonefish in the Arabian Gulf which occurs in very shallow water, often being found in tide pools (only 4–5 cms in depth) at low tide. Prefers rocky areas interspersed with patches of sand or sand-mud bottom. The Black-mouth stonefish can be distinguished from *Synanceja verrucosa* by its black mouth and black-edged pectoral fins. The centre of the pectoral fins is salmon-pink, and these fins are flared as a defence, or warning, posture when the fish is disturbed. This fish should be considered dangerous. Length: 20 cms.

Synanceja verrucosa (Bloch and Schneider)
Reef stonefish
Known from the UAE; Africa to Hawaii.

This extremely dangerous stonefish is perhaps less common in the Arabian Gulf than the former species, and can be distinguished by its white mouth and even more 'rock-like' appearance. Length: 30 cms.

Family PLATYCEPHALIDAE

Flatheads are Indo-Pacific fishes which frequent shallow coastal waters and estuaries. Voracious predators. Reproduction involves production of small pelagic eggs. Characterised by dorso-ventrally flattened bodies, large mouth, and two dorsal fins, the first with 6–9 spines. Coloration is usually light brown, or mottled brown and white, adaptations for concealment when the fish buries into sand or sand-mud bottoms. There are perhaps three species in the Arabian Gulf.

Platycephalus indicus (Linnaeus)
                                    Bar-tailed flathead (Plate III)
Throughout Arabian Gulf; Africa to Japan.

This is the most common Gulf species and is encountered in shallow water over sand or sand-mud substrates close to shorelines. The most obvious characteristic of this species is the yellow- or cream-coloured tail with three white-edged black streaks. These fish lie partially buried and well camouflaged in the substrate with mouth directed upward and consume small fish and invertebrates. Important food fish. Length: 1 m.

Other species
Two other less common flatheads, *Platycephalus maculipinna* Regan and *P. tuberculatus* Cuvier and Valenciennes, have been recorded from the Arabian Gulf. The former is distinguished by the dark, unstriped tail and a black blotch in the first dorsal fin. The second species is a more deep-water fish characterised by an unstriped tail with small brown spots. Little is known of either species.

Order **PERCIFORMES**

Marine and freshwater. Most diverse bony-fish order with many families. Two dorsal fins, sometimes continuous or separated only by a shallow notch. Spines in the dorsal and anal fins. One spine in each pelvic fin. Scales, if present, are rough (ctenoid). Pelvic fins located in the chest region or the throat region. More than thirty families in inshore waters of the Arabian Gulf.

Family SERRANIDAE

Sea bass and groupers are marine fish of all tropical and temperate seas, and often attain a very large size. Found on rock substrates, especially coral reefs. Carnivorous. Excellent food fishes of great commercial significance. Some species produce floating non-adhesive eggs, and others sticky eggs which sink (demersal eggs). The condition of hermaphroditism, both sexes present in the same individual, is common. Characterised by a large mouth, three spines on the operculum, small scales, a rounded or truncate caudal fin, rounded pectoral fins, a long dorsal fin in which the spinous portion and soft ray portion are continuous, and three anal fin spines. There are about five common inshore species in the Arabian Gulf but they are often difficult to identify.

Cephalopholis miniatus (Forskål)   Blue-spotted grouper
Throughout Arabian Gulf; Red Sea to Australia.
   Body red-brown with numerous blue spots. The blue spots are rimmed with black. Tail rounded. Length: 45 cms.

a

b

c

d

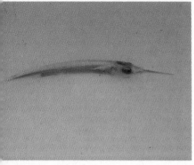

e

PLATE I
a   *Rhinobatos granulatus*
b   *Rhynchobatos djiddensis*
    (dorsal view)
c   *Rhynchobatos djiddensis*
    (ventral view)
d   *Chirocentrus dorab*
e   *Hyporhamphus sindensis*

a

b

c

d

PLATE II
a   *Aphanius dispar* (male)
b   *Aphanius dispar* (male and female)
c   *Allanetta forskåli*
d   *Centriscus scutatus*

a

b

c

d

PLATE III
a   *Pseudosynanceia melanostigma*
b   *Platycephalus indicus*
c   *Epinephelus tauvina*
d   *Pseudochromis dutoiti*

a

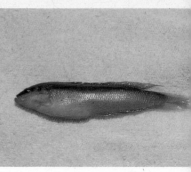

b

c

d

e

PLATE IV
a *Pseudochromis persicus*
   (dark phase)
b *Pseudochromis persicus*
   (light phase)
c *Therapon theraps*
d *Apogonichthys nigripinnis*
e *Sillago sihama*

a

b

c

d

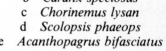

e

PLATE V
a   *Atropus atropus*
b   *Caranx speciosus*
c   *Chorinemus lysan*
d   *Scolopsis phaeops*
e   *Acanthopagrus bifasciatus*

a

b

c

d

PLATE VI
a   *Diplodus noct*
b   *Upeneus tragula*
c   *Chaetodon obscurus*
d   *Heniochus acuminatus*

a

b

c

d

e

PLATE VII
a   *Pristotis jerdoni*
b   *Mugil macrolepis*
c   *Polydactylus sextarius*
d   *Bathygobius fuscus*
e   *Boleophthalmus boddarti*

a

b

c

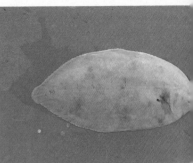
d

PLATE VIII
a   *Periophthalmus koelreuteri*
b   *Scartelaos viridis*
c   *Siganus oramin*
d   *Synaptura orientalis*

Epinephelus areolatus (Forskål) Yellow-spotted rock cod
Throughout Arabian Gulf; Africa to East Indies, Australia.

Variable in characteristics, but recognisable by the lunate tail. Coloration consists of red-brown spots on the body and all fins. The spots may sometimes appear yellowish. Background coloration is blue-white. Length: 40 cms.

Epinephelus chlorostigma (Cuvier and Valenciennes)
Hexagon grouper
Throughout Arabian Gulf; Africa to China.

Hexagonal brown body markings and nearly square tail. Length: 60 cms.

Epinephelus diacanthus (Cuvier and Valenciennes)
Six-barred reef cod
Recorded from Iraq, but probably occurs throughout the Arabian Gulf; Indo-Pacific.

Six prominent vertical bars on the body and two stout spines on the preoperculum.

Epinephelus tauvina (Forskål)
Rock cod, or Hamoor (Plate III)
Throughout Arabian Gulf; Africa to Hawaii.

This is the best known and most commonly encountered grouper of the Arabian Gulf, and is one of the most prized food fishes. A variable species, *E. tauvina* is most readily distinguished by the small dark brown or rust-coloured spots all over the body and head. The tail is rounded. Adults are a more uniform rust-brown colour than are juveniles. An aggressive fish which may be dangerous when large. Length: 2 m.

Other species
On the basis of known Indo-Pacific distribution, a number of other serranid fishes may be expected to occur in the Arabian Gulf, especially in deeper water and on coral

reefs. A list of such species would include perhaps as many as twenty species.

Family PSEUDOCHROMIDAE

Dottybacks are marine fishes of the Indo-Pacific region. They are small relatives of the sea bass and groupers (Serranidae), and are sometimes classified with them. Carnivorous fish of rock substrates, especially coral reefs. Characterised by a single long dorsal fin with three spines. The lateral line has two portions: an anterior portion from the operculum along the body just beneath the dorsal fin, and a posterior portion on the caudal peduncle. Four species known in the Arabian Gulf.

Pseudochromis dutoiti Smith
Orange dottyback (Plate III)
Known from Kuwait, Saudi Arabia and Bahrain; Africa to Sri Lanka.

A colourful and conspicuous fish of rock substrates, especially coral reefs. Has been found in shallow water (less than 2 m in depth) to depths of 25 m. The body of this easily recognised fish is orange to nearly red with an electric blue stripe from the snout through the eye and along the sides just below the dorsal fin. The orange caudal fin is bordered with blue. Length: 7 cms.

Pseudochromis nigrovittatus Boulenger   dottyback
Oman and Mekran coast.

The existence of this fish in the Arabian Gulf remains to be verified. Two specimens from the Arabian Gulf are known, but the precise locality is not known. Lubbock (1975), in his study of the genus *Pseudochromis*, did not find the species in Bahrain, Abu Dhabi or Saudi Arabia. Likewise, it has not been found in Kuwait or Iran. The original specimens may well have come from outside the Strait of Hormuz. This dottyback is similar in appearance to the light-colour phase of *P. persicus* (see below), but can

66

be distinguished from that species in that the black stripe from the snout through the eye and onto the body extends to the middle caudal fin rays. In *P. persicus* the stripe extends to the upper portion of the tail. Length: 6 cms.

Pseudochromis olivaceus Rüppell   dottyback
Known from Saudi Arabia and Abu Dhabi; Red Sea, Arabian Gulf, Gulf of Aden.

Found on coral reefs. Distinguished by olive-coloured body with yellow abdomen. There is a blue spot on the operculum, and the dorsal fin has a red margin. Length: 6·5 cms.

Pseudochromis persicus Murray
               Persian Gulf dottyback (Plate IV)
Kuwait, Saudi Arabia, Bahrain; Arabian Gulf and northern Arabian Sea.

Generally distributed over rock rubble and coral substrates throughout the Gulf, and one of the most conspicuous and common rocky-substrate fishes in shallow water. There are two colour phases: a dark blue to black phase (entire body and dorsal, anal and caudal fins) with orange-pink pectoral fins, and a lighter phase, cream-coloured, with a dark stripe from the snout through the eye and onto the body and extending to the upper portion of the tail. This latter phase has clear fins. Both colour phases have small, bright blue spots all over the body and unpaired fins. These colour phases appear not to be correlated with sexual differences. Mature females, of either colour phase, may have pinkish abdomens, an indication of the orange-pink coloured eggs internally. Small crabs are a major food item. Length: 12 cms.

Family THERAPONIDAE

Small relatives of the groupers and sea bass, the theraponids are found in marine and brackish waters of the Indo-Pacific region. Carnivorous. Edible. Characterised by an elongate body, small mouth (at least compared to groupers), a deep notch between the spiny and soft parts of the dorsal fin and 1–2 spines on the operculum. The edge of the preoperculum is saw-toothed (serrate). Scales are rough (ctenoid). Longitudinal stripes on body. Probably five species in the Arabian Gulf.

Helotes sexlineatus (Quoy and Gaimard)

Striped therapon

Throughout Arabian Gulf; Africa to China.

This species has apparently been confused with *Pelates quadrilineatus* in earlier studies of Arabian Gulf fishes. It is, however, a common and distinct species. Characterised by 4–6 longitudinal stripes from head to tail and a large dark blotch on the shoulder. The outer (distal) half of the dorsal fin is dark. The tail is slightly forked and has three vertical, dark bands, one at the base, one in the middle, and another on the posterior rim of the fin. Length: 25 cms.

Pelates quadrilineatus (Bloch)   Trumpeter perch

Throughout Arabian Gulf; Arabian Gulf to East Indies, Australia.

This species has been confused with the preceding one, which it resembles closely. Body markings are similar to *H. sexlineatus*, but the tail is unmarked and the outer half of the dorsal fin is not dark. There is a dark blotch in the spinous portion of the dorsal fin. Length: 20 cms.

Therapon jarbua (Forskål)   Crescent perch

Known with certainty from the southern Gulf, but probably occurs throughout; Indo-Pacific.

Distinguished by three longitudinal lines on the body. The two lower lines angle sharply upward above the pectoral fins to the area between the head and first dorsal fin. Dark spot in the spinous dorsal fin. Tail forked, dark-tipped and with three longitudinal stripes. Known to spawn in estuaries. Length: 25 cms.

Therapon puta (Cuvier and Valenciennes)
banded therapon
Throughout Arabian Gulf; Red Sea to East Indies, Philippines.

Common. Characterised by two conspicuous longitudinal stripes, one from the middle of the eye to the base of the tail fin, and another from above the eye to the posterior base of the second dorsal fin. A fainter stripe also occurs both above and below these prominent stripes. Tail slightly forked and with 3–5 faint longitudinal stripes. Slender body. Length: 20 cms.

Therapon theraps (Cuvier and Valenciennes)
banded therapon (Plate IV)
Throughout Arabian Gulf; Africa to Australia.

Characterised by four wide longitudinal bands. Deeper-bodied than other therapons. Large, dark blotch in the spinous dorsal fin. The forked caudal fin has four longitudinal stripes, two on the upper lobe of the fin and two on the lower. The upper tip of the caudal fin is black. Length: 20 cms.

Family APOGONIDAE

Cardinalfishes are small fishes of warm marine waters throughout the world, both in shallow and deep water. Some occur in estuaries, but most are found on coral reefs. Eggs are incubated orally in most species. Nocturnal, but can be seen in crevices, under ledges or amongst the protective spines of sea urchins during the day. Carnivorous. Small fishes of no economic value. Characterised by two separate dorsal fins, the first with 6–9 spines and the second with 8–14 rays. Anal fin with 2–3 spines and 7–18 rays. Mouth and head large. Coloration usually red; often colourful fishes. At least five species may be encountered in shallow, inshore waters in the Arabian Gulf. Additional species can be expected.

Apogon quadrifasciatus Cuvier
                              Four-banded cardinalfish
Throughout Arabian Gulf; Africa to East Indies, Australia, Taiwan.

A common species around coral reefs. Two silvery bands on sides, each bordered with black, giving a four-lined appearance. One band continues onto the tail. Length: 10 cms.

Apogonichthys nigripinnis (Cuvier and Valenciennes)
                              One-spot cardinalfish (Plate IV)
= *Apogon thurstoni* Day and *Apogon uninotatus* (Smith and Radcliffe)

Throughout Arabian Gulf; Africa to East Indies.

The most often encountered cardinalfish in the Arabian Gulf. It inhabits rock ledges, coral reefs, rock rubble in shallow water, the spines of long-spined sea urchins and even grass beds. Distinguished by a large, round, dark spot (ocellus) bordered by a light ring, between the pectoral fin and spinous dorsal fin. This species is the *Apogon uninotatus* and *A. thurstoni* of other workers in the Arabian Gulf, but these are all surely the same fish.

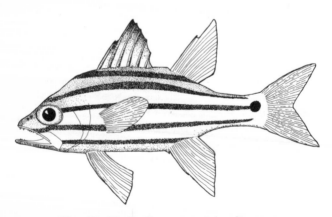

Fig. 15 *Cheilodipterus quinquelineatus*

Cheilodipterus quinquelineatus Cuvier and
Valenciennes   Five-line cardinalfish (Fig. 15)
= *Paramia quinquelineata* (Cuvier and Valenciennes)
    Throughout Arabian Gulf; Africa to Tahiti.
    A common and conspicuous cardinalfish of coral reefs.
Generally seen in large schools under ledges. The most
distinguishing characteristics are the five dark lines on the
head and body. There is a yellow spot with a dark centre at
the base of the tail. Length: 10 cms.

Lovamia novemfasciata Cuvier and Valenciennes
                            Nine-banded cardinalfish
= *Apogon novemfasciata* (Cuvier and Valenciennes)
    Reported, tentatively, from the southern Arabian Gulf;
Indian Ocean.
    Four or five broad longitudinal stripes from the snout to
the base of the caudal fin. No spot at the base of the tail fin.
Length: 7 cms.

Pristiapogon fraenatus (Valenciennes)
                            Spiny-eyed cardinalfish
= *Apogon fraenatus* Valenciennes
    Known from numerous localities along the Iranian
coast, and probably occurs throughout the Arabian Gulf;
Africa to Polynesia.
    A broad lateral stripe from the snout through the eye to
the base of the caudal fin, where it terminates as a round
spot. Colour pinkish. Length: 8 cms.

Family SILLAGINIDAE

Whitings are Indo-Pacific fishes found in shallow coastal
waters, usually over sand bottoms. These carnivorous fish
feed by probing into the sand for small invertebrates.
Elongate fish with a slightly forked tail, small mouth and
rough (ctenoid) scales. The two dorsal fins are separated by
a notch. Coloration is light yellow to silvery. One species in
the Arabian Gulf.

71

Sillago sihama (Forskål)   Southern whiting (Plate IV)
Throughout Arabian Gulf; Africa to Australia.
  Very abundant in shallow waters along sandy beaches.
Forms schools of 4–6 individuals. Known to produce
pelagic eggs. A good food fish. Length: 30 cms.

Family RACHYCENTRIDAE

There is only one species of Cobia, and it is found both in
the Atlantic and Indo-Pacific seas. Predator. A well-
known game and food fish. The Cobia is an elongate fish
with a somewhat flattened head (resembles a remora – see
below – but without suction disc). Scales are small. A
unique feature which provides easy recognition is the
presence of 6–9 free spines before the dorsal fin.

Rachycentron canadus (Linnaeus)   Cobia
Throughout Arabian Gulf; world-wide.
  Found on coral reefs and offshore. Length: 1·5 m.

Family ECHENEIDAE

Remoras, or shark suckers, are marine fishes of all seas,
being found wherever there are sharks or other large
fishes, sea turtles or marine mammals to attach to. Characterised by a flattened head with a suction disc. Remoras get
a free ride on their hosts and pieces of food left over from
the feeding habits of the host. The host may benefit by
having parasites cleaned from its surface by the remora.
Produce pelagic eggs. One species known from the
Arabian Gulf.

Echeneis naucrates Linnaeus   remora (Fig. 16)
Throughout Arabian Gulf; found in all seas.
  The suction disc on the head readily distinguishes this
species from all other fishes in the Gulf. Length: 1 m.

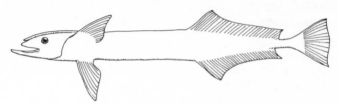

Fig. 16 *Echeneis naucrates*

Family CARANGIDAE

Jacks, trevallies, and pompanos are marine fishes of all seas. They often form large schools and may be found both close to shorelines and far offshore. Fast-swimming predators, jacks are excellent game and food fishes. Produce pelagic eggs. The body form ranges from slender to deep-bodied. Scales, except for scutes on the caudal peduncle of some species, are small, and the body is therefore smooth. The most distinctive feature of carangids is that the first two anal fin spines are detached from the rest of the fin. Two dorsal fins. Caudal peduncle slender and caudal fin forked. Pectoral fin elongate and often scythe-like (falcate). There are probably more than twenty species of carangids in the Arabian Gulf, of which less than ten are common inshore species.

Alectis indicus (Rüppell)   Indian trevally
Throughout Arabian Gulf; Indo-Pacific.
   Spines of dorsal fin separate towards tips, and are small. Rays of dorsal and anal fins prolonged as filaments. Pelvic fins black. Body diamond-shaped and compressed laterally. Length: 1 m.

Atropus atropus (Bloch and Schneider)
                                   trevally (Plate V)
Throughout Arabian Gulf; Africa to China.
   First dorsal fin normal in shape. Rays of dorsal and anal fin prolonged as filaments, as in *Alectis*. Pelvic fins black. Body somewhat rounder than *Alectis*. Length: 25 cms.

73

Caranx chrysophrys (Cuvier and Valenciennes)
Long-nosed trevally
Throughout Arabian Gulf; Africa to Melanesia.
Distinguished by 25–30 weak scutes on lateral line, 19–20 dorsal fin rays, 15–16 anal fin rays, and large spot on the operculum. Second dorsal fin and anal fin falcate. Length: 50 cms.

Caranx djedaba Forskål   trevally
Throughout Arabian Gulf; Africa to Taiwan.
Back blue with 6–10 cross bars. Large opercular spot. Anterior part of lateral line markedly arched upward. 45–50 lateral scutes. Length: 20 cms.

Caranx gymnostethoides Bleeker   jack
Known from the UAE; Africa to Hawaii.
Grey colour; bronze-green fins. No scales on breast. 25 lateral scutes. Length: 90 cms.

Caranx ignobilis (Forskål)   Yellow-fin jack, or trevally
Known from Saudi Arabia and the UAE; Africa to Hawaii.
Olive green with yellow fins. No spot on operculum. No scales on breast. About 30 lateral scutes. Length: 1·5 m.

Caranx kalla Cuvier and Valenciennes   Herring trevally
Throughout Arabian Gulf; Africa to Hawaii.
Green on back, shading to yellow on sides and abdomen. About seven faint cross bars on body. 40–48 lateral scutes. Length: 20 cms.

Caranx leptolepis (Cuvier)   Yellow-banded trevally
Throughout Arabian Gulf; Indo-Pacific.
Elongate. Colour blue with a yellow band from the shoulder to the area beneath the second dorsal fin. 25–33 lateral scutes. Length: 18 cms.

Caranx malabaricus (Bloch and Schneider)
Malabar trevally
Throughout Arabian Gulf; Africa to Melanesia.
Very similar in appearance to *Caranx chrysophrys*, but
with 21–24 dorsal fin rays and 17–19 anal fin rays. Length:
40 cms.

Caranx mate (Cuvier and Valenciennes) jack
Known from the UAE; Africa to Hawaii.
Blue-green colour on back shading to silver on sides and
abdomen. Scales on breast. 40–50 lateral scutes. Length:
29 cms.

Caranx speciosus (Forskål) Golden trevally (Plate V)
Throughout Arabian Gulf; Africa to Hawaii.
A very distinctive fish with a golden body and 10–12 dark
vertical bars. Fins yellow. Tips of tail black. 15–25 lateral
scutes. Length: 1·2 m.

Chorinemus lysan (Forskål)
Spotted leatherskin, or queenfish (Plate V)
Throughout Arabian Gulf; Arabia to Melanesia.
Silvery, elongate fish easily recognised by five to seven
thumbprint-like spots above the lateral line. The first dorsal fin consists of seven well-separated spines. No scutes on
sides and scales very small. Mouth large. Length: 1 m.

Chorinemus sancti-petri Cuvier and Valenciennes
queenfish
Known from southern Arabian Gulf, but probably occurs
throughout; Africa to Hawaii.
Silvery, elongate fish which resembles *C. lysan*, but is
distinguishable from that species by six to ten round spots
above the lateral line and three to five below. The soft
(second) dorsal fin has a black spot. Length: 1·2 m.

Decapterus russelli (Rüppell) scad
Known from the UAE; Indo-Pacific.

Elongate, silvery, 40–45 scutes on each side. Length: 20 cms.

Elagatis bipinnulatus (Quoy and Gaimard)
Rainbow runner
Known from southern Arabian Gulf, but probably occurs throughout; Africa to Hawaii.

Elongate. Spinous dorsal fin continuous with the soft dorsal fin. There are small detached 'finlets' between the soft dorsal fin and the tail, and between the anal fin and the tail. Golden longitudinal stripe bordered by blue stripes. Good game and food fish. Usually an offshore species. Length: 1 m.

Megalaspis cordyla (Linnaeus)   Finny scad
Known from the UAE; Africa to Hawaii.

Elongate. Dorsal and anal fins followed by ten finlets. Dorsal fin black-edged. More than 50 scutes. Length: 45 cms.

Naucrates ductor (Linnaeus)   Pilotfish
Probably throughout Arabian Gulf; world-wide in tropical seas.

Dorsal fin and anal fin spines weak. Anal spines may be reduced or absent in older individuals. Back blue; abdomen silvery. Five to seven black bands on body. Associates with sharks. Length: 60 cms.

Trachinotus bailonii (Lacépède)
Black-spotted swallowtail
Recorded from the Strait of Hormuz, its distribution in the Arabian Gulf is unclear; Africa to Melanesia.

Spines of dorsal fin separate. Soft dorsal fin and anal fin markedly falcate. Three to six dark spots on lateral line. No scutes. Length: 60 cms.

Trachinotus blochii (Lacépède) Pompano, or swallowtail
Saudi Arabia and the UAE; Africa to Melanesia.

Spines of dorsal fin separate. Soft dorsal and anal fins falcate. Similar to *T. bailonii*, but lacks spots on sides. Length: 90 cms.

Zonichthys nigrofasciata (Rüppell)

Dark-banded yellowtail

= *Seriola nigrofasciata* (Rüppell)

Throughout Arabian Gulf; Africa to Melanesia.

Found more offshore. Elongate. Dark-coloured. Young with five to seven vertical bands. Ridge on caudal peduncle. Length: 90 cms.

Family MENIDAE

This family is represented by only one species, *Mene maculata*. Forms large schools. Edible. Easily recognised by deep body which is laterally very thin, small scales, narrow caudal peduncle, and forked tail. The mouth is directed upward.

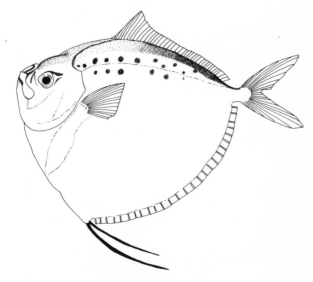

Fig. 17 *Mene maculata*

77

Mene maculata (Bloch and Schneider)

Moonfish (Fig. 17)

Throughout Arabian Gulf; Africa to Australia, Melanesia.
   Most likely to be encountered around coral reefs or in
deeper water. Length: 20 cms.

Family LEIOGNATHIDAE

Ponyfishes, or slipmouths, are Indo-Pacific fishes found in
marine and brackish water. Form schools in shallow water.
Eaten after being dried. Produce pelagic eggs. Characterised by highly extendable mouths, and a single long
dorsal fin. The anterior portion of the dorsal fin bears eight
to nine spines. The anal and dorsal fins can be folded into a
sheath at the base of each fin. Scales are very small and the
body is slimy. The caudal peduncle is narrow and the tail is
forked. At least seven species occur in the Arabian Gulf.

Leiognathus bindus (Valenciennes)

Orange-finned slipmouth

Throughout Arabian Gulf; Arabian Gulf to East Indies.
   A fairly common Gulf species, the orange-finned slipmouth is characterised by yellow-orange fins and a black
line along the base of the dorsal fin. The lateral line continues onto the caudal fin. Length: 8 cms.

Leiognathus daurus Cuvier   ponyfish
Recorded from the southern Arabian Gulf and coast of
Iran; Arabian Gulf to Australia.
   Characterised by a conspicuous, dark triangular spot
between the top of the head and the dorsal fin. The dorsal
fin has orange spots. Length: 8 cms.

Leiognathus equulus (Forskål)   Common ponyfish
Recorded from Iraq in the Shatt-al-Arab; Africa to
Melanesia.

Lateral line extends onto the caudal fin. Four yellow blotches under the lateral line on the sides are a distinctive feature. Length: 25 cms.

Leiognathus fasciatus (Lacépède)   Banded ponyfish
Throughout Arabian Gulf; Arabian Gulf to East Indies, Melanesia, Tahiti.
   Distinguished by an elongate second dorsal spine which is produced into a filament. The lateral line ends before the caudal fin base. Length: 15 cms.

Leiognathus insidiator (Bloch)
                              Slender ponyfish (Fig. 18)
Throughout Arabian Gulf; Africa to Tahiti.
   A markedly oblique mouth. Spinous dorsal fin tipped with black. Length: 10 cms.

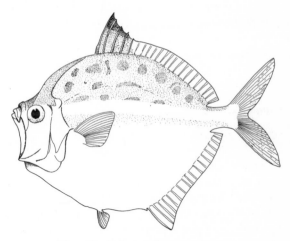

Fig. 18 *Leiognathus insidiator*

Leiognathus lineolatus Cuvier   Lined ponyfish (Fig. 19)
Southern Arabian Gulf; Arabian Gulf to Japan.
   An elongate species with dark spots, irregular in place-ment, on the silvery body. Length: 12 cms.

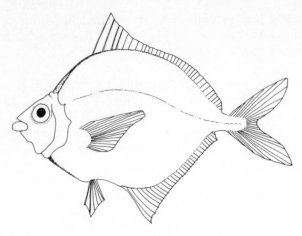

Fig. 19 *Leiognathus equulus*

Leiognathus splendens (Cuvier)   Splendid ponyfish
Recorded from Iraq; Arabian Gulf to Tahiti.
    Mouth horizontal. Spinous dorsal fin tipped with black.
Length: 13 cms.

Family LUTJANIDAE

Snappers are a marine, circumtropical family of large,
edible species. A few species enter brackish estuaries. All
species are carnivores and important food fishes. Pelagic
eggs are produced. A continuous dorsal fin, large mouth,
and enlarged canine teeth characterise these fish. Often
very colourful. At least fifteen species occur in the Arabian
Gulf and the taxonomy, distribution and habits of these
valuable fishes are poorly known. Only common inshore
species are considered here.

Lutjanus coccineus (Cuvier and Valenciennes)
                                        Crimson snapper
Throughout Arabian Gulf; Africa to East Indies.
    A very common Gulf species, but is found more offshore
and on coral reefs. Seen frequently in fish markets. The

name *Lutjanus sanguineus* may have also been used for this species, and a very similar species, *L. gibbus*, may also occur in the Arabian Gulf, These fish have a bright pink coloration. Length: 50 cms.

Lutjanus fulviflamma (Forskål)   One-spot snapper
Throughout Arabian Gulf; Africa to Japan, Polynesia.

A common Gulf species, especially around coral reefs and rocky areas. This species and *L. johni* are very similar and often difficult to distinguish. The characteristic black spot on the sides is mostly below the lateral line in *L. fulviflamma*, and its margins are indistinct. Length: 30 cms.

Lutjanus johni (Bloch and Schneider)
                              Golden-striped snapper
Throughout Arabian Gulf; Africa to Polynesia.

Common. The black spot on the body is mostly above the lateral line. Length: 35 cms.

Lutjanus kasmira (Forskål)
                              Blue-striped snapper (Fig. 20)
Throughout Arabian Gulf; Africa to Hawaii.

Common. Similar to *L. johni* in that the black spot on the sides is mostly above the lateral line, but can be dis-

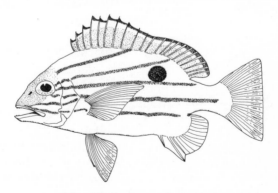

Fig. 20 *Lutjanus kasmira*

81

tinguished from that species by the five electric blue stripes that extend from head to tail. The black spot lies between the second and third stripes. The head tends to be yellow. Length: 35 cms.

Lutjanus lineolatus (Rüppell)
Golden-striped red snapper

Throughout Arabian Gulf; Africa to Melanesia.

May not be common. Characterised by several longitudinal golden stripes on sides, but particularly by one conspicuous golden stripe from the eye to the base of the caudal fin. Length: 35 cms.

Other species recorded from the Arabian Gulf

Aprion microlepis (Bleeker): Posterior dorsal and anal fin rays extend as filaments. Red colour.

Aprion virescens Cuvier and Valenciennes: Bluish colour. Posterior rays of dorsal and anal fins extended as filaments.

Lutjanus. argentimaculatus (Forskål): Dark red-brown colour dorsally and red on abdomen. Found on coral reefs.

Lutjanus duodecimlineatus (Cuvier and Valenciennes): Similar to *L. kasmira*, but lacks black spot on side. Rocky areas.

Lutjanus ehrenbergi (Peters): Similar to *L. fulviflamma* and *L. johni*, but may not actually occur in the Arabian Gulf.

Lutjanus janthinopterus (Bleeker): Numerous yellow stripes on body. Yellow fins with black margins. Tail black. Coral reef inhabitant.

Lutjanus rangus (Cuvier and Valenciennes): Green head. Body and fins golden.

Lutjanus rivulatus (Cuvier and Valenciennes): A deepbodied snapper with orange-tipped fins, a white-bordered ocellus on the sides, and light blue spots in each body scale.

Lutjanus russelli (Bleeker): Similar to *L. fulviflamma*, but with more dorsal fin rays (14–15, as against 13 in *L. fulviflamma*). Coral reefs.

Lutjanus vaigensis (Quoy and Gaimard): Six or more golden stripes on body.

Family NEMIPTERIDAE

Threadfins are Indo-Pacific marine fishes of small to moderate size which are usually found around coral reefs. These fishes are carnivores and considered good to eat. Elongate bodies. Distinguished most readily from snappers (Lutjanidae), to which they appear to be closely related, by the lack of teeth on the roof of the mouth (palatine and vomerine teeth). Five common species in the Arabian Gulf.

Nemipterus japonicus (Bloch and Schneider)
                                        Threadfin bream
Throughout Arabian Gulf; Arabian Gulf to Japan.
    A common Arabian Gulf species characterised by an elongate filament which extends from the upper lobe of the caudal fin, a feature shared with *N. tolu*. Differs from *N. tolu* in that it has eight yellowish lines on its light red body, as opposed to the four or five such lines in *N. tolu*. Length: 25 cms.

Nemipterus tolu (Cuvier and Valenciennes)
                                        Butterfly bream
Throughout Arabian Gulf; Arabian Gulf to East Indies.
    A common Arabian Gulf species. Characteristics used to distinguish it from *N. japonicus* are given with the description of that species. Rosy-red colour. Length: 25 cms.

Scolopsis ghanam (Forskål)   Peppered grunt
Throughout Arabian Gulf; East Africa to Melanesia.
    Common around coral reefs, but is not often seen on rock substrates close to shore. A light line extends from above the eye to the end of the first dorsal fin, and another extends from the eye to the edge of the operculum and continues to the caudal peduncle. Length: 20 cms.

Scolopsis personatus (Cuvier and Valenciennes)   grunt
Recorded from near Bahrain, but occurrence in the
Arabian Gulf should be verified; Arabian Gulf to Austra-
lia.

A white stripe from the eye to the caudal peduncle and a
white, or blue-white, bar between the eyes distinguish this
species from other *Scolopsis*. Length: 25 cms.

Scolopsis phaeops (Bennett)
                              Blue-cheeked grunt (Plate V)
Throughout Arabian Gulf; Arabian Gulf to East Indies.

This is the most commonly observed grunt in shallow
water in the Arabian Gulf. It is an inquisitive fish which will
swim up to a skin diver. Prefers rocky areas and coral reefs.
Recognised easily by the bluish-white line at the base of the
dorsal fin. Dorsal and caudal fins are dark. Length: 35 cms.

Family GERREIDAE

Mojarras, or sand perch, are marine and brackish-water
fishes found throughout the tropical and sub-tropical seas
of the world. They inhabit shallow, sand bottom areas and
estuaries, and eat small invertebrates. Edible, but tend to
be small and bony. Characterised by an extendable mouth,
a single dorsal fin and a deeply forked tail. There is a scaly
sheath along the base of the dorsal and anal fins. Silver
colour. Three common species in the Arabian Gulf.

Gerres filamentosus Cuvier and Valenciennes
                              Long-finned mojarra (Fig. 21)
= *Gerres punctatus* Cuvier and Valenciennes
    Throughout Arabian Gulf; Africa to Japan.

The most common Arabian Gulf mojarra. Found along
sandy beaches and inlets. Possesses a greatly elongate
second dorsal spine (most pronounced in adults). Pectoral
fins are long, extending back to the anal opening. There are
about ten faint vertical lines, often broken up into a series
of spots, on the sides. The snout may be black in adults.

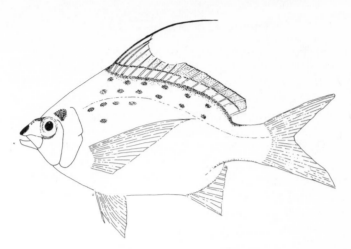

Fig. 21 *Gerres filamentosus*

Juveniles are silvery and may be difficult to distinguish from the next species. Length: 20 cms.

Gerres oyena (Forskål)   mojarra
Throughout Arabian Gulf; Africa to Australia.

Similar to *G. filamentosus*, but lacks the elongate dorsal filament, and is silvery with no spots or vertical lines, although some adults may show faint vertical lines. Pectoral fins do not extend as far back as the anal opening. It is likely that studies of Arabian Gulf fishes have not clearly distinguished between these two species. Juveniles of both species of *Gerres* are similar. The number of lateral scales, 45 or more in *G. filamentosus*, and less than 40 in *G. oyena*, is also a distinguishing feature. Length: 20 cms.

Pentaprion longimanus (Cantor)   mojarra
Throughout Arabian Gulf; Indian Ocean.

A more offshore fish. First and second dorsal fins are nearly separated by a deep notch. The body is elongate and silvery, with an intense silver stripe from the operculum to the base of the caudal fin. Anal fin long. Length: 20 cms.

Family POMADASYIDAE

Grunts are a large group of moderate-size marine fishes found in both the Atlantic and the Indo-Pacific region. They are usually found in rocky areas and on coral reefs. Carnivorous. Good to eat. Produce pelagic eggs. Characterised by a continuous dorsal fin with ten spines and eight or nine rays. Teeth are small and needle-like, and there are no enlarged canine teeth as in snappers. There are no teeth on the roof of the mouth. No opercular spine. Generally resemble snappers. Coloration is variable from species to species and changes from juvenile to adult. About twelve species in the Arabian Gulf, eight of which may be encountered inshore.

Plectorhynchus cinctus (Temminck and Schlegel)

Three-banded grunt

Throughout Arabian Gulf; Arabian Gulf to Japan.

Common. Numerous large spots on body, mostly above the lateral line. Dorsal and caudal fins also with large spots. Spots on sides may coalesce to form three lateral stripes. Tail round. Length: 60 cms.

Plectorhynchus gaterinus (Forskål)   Spotted gaterin

Southern Arabian Gulf; Arabian Gulf to Africa.

Juveniles have seven or eight stripes on the body from the snout to the tail, and dorsal, anal and caudal fins are yellow with one or more rows of spots. Adults are heavily spotted all over the body (except head) and median fins. Length: 40 cms.

Plectorhynchus lineatus (Linnaeus)

Yellow-banded sweetlips, or Striped gaterin

= *Gaterin lineatus* (Linnaeus)

Southern Arabian Gulf; Arabian Gulf to Melanesia.

Yellow and black stripes on body from head to tail. Dorsal and pelvic fins yellow. Length: 35 cms.

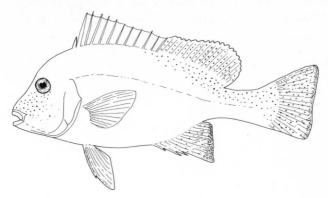

Fig. 22 *Plectorhynchus pictus*

Plectorhynchus pictus (Thunberg)
  Painted grunt, or Painted sweetlips (Fig. 22)
= *Spiloptichthys pictus* (Thunberg)
  Throughout Arabian Gulf; Africa to Polynesia, Japan.
  Very common. Frequents coral reefs. Juveniles can be identified by the prominent, dark body stripes, variable in number (depends on size), from the head to (and including) the tail. The anal and pelvic fins also bear a prominent stripe. Adults are grey-brown with dark fins. Some large spots occur on the caudal fin and along the base of the dorsal fin. Length: 45 cms.

Plectorhynchus schotaf (Forskål)
  Grey grunt, or Grey sweetlips
  Throughout Arabian Gulf; Africa to East Indies, Australia.
  Common. Uniform grey colour. Lacks dark spots on body. Fins are dusky or grey, especially the dorsal and caudal fins. Length: 80 cms.

Pomadasys argyreus (Cuvier and Valenciennes)
  Silver grunt
= *P. argenteus* (Forskål)
  Throughout Arabian Gulf; Africa to East Indies.

87

Common. Silvery fish with a large dark blotch on the operculum behind the eye. Length: 50 cms.

Pomadasys maculatus (Bloch)   Blotched grunt
Southern Arabian Gulf; Africa to Melanesia.
   Body with several dark blotches, or incomplete vertical bars. A dark blotch on the spinous portion of the dorsal fin. Length: 45 cms.

Pomadasys opercularis (Playfair)   Spotted grunt
Recorded from the southern Arabian Gulf; Africa to Australia, East Indies.
   Probably not a common inshore species. Numerous small spots on the body and dorsal fin. Length: 40 cms.

Rhoniscus stridens (Forskål)   grunt
Throughout Arabian Gulf; Africa to the Indian Ocean.
   Best known in the southern Gulf. Dark stripe from the eye to the base of the soft dorsal fin, and a black spot just behind the operculum. Length: 45 cms.

Family LETHRINIDAE *SCAVENGERS*

Lethrinids are wide-ranging, marine, coastal fishes of the Indo-Pacific region and west coast of Africa, and are especially common around coral reefs. All are carnivores and are considered good food fishes. They have a single continuous dorsal fin with ten spines and about nine soft rays. The top of the head and preoperculum are scaleless, the operculum has scales, the tail is slightly forked, lips are thick and fleshy, and there are canine teeth and molar-like teeth in the mouth. Colour patterns vary considerably from species to species, and are the best diagnostic features as species are otherwise not easily identified. Four or five species are known from the Arabian Gulf, but identifications are tenuous, and other species may be found.

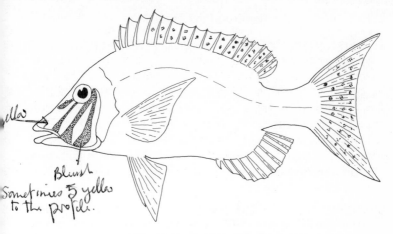

yella

Bluish
Sometimes 5 yellow
to the profile.

Fig. 23 *Lethrinus nebulosus*

Lethrinus nebulosus (Forskål)   Pig-face bream (Fig. 23)
Throughout Arabian Gulf; Red Sea to Australia.
    Probably the most common Arabian Gulf lethrinid, and
the species most likely to be encountered around coral
reefs or, as juveniles, along shallow coastlines and in inlets.
An olive-green fish, lighter ventrally, with a pale blue spot
in the centre of each body scale. Fins pinkish with pale blue
spots. Adults may have blue lines radiating from the eye. A
valuable food fish. Length: 75 cms.

Other species
Lethrinus fletus Whitley: Has been recorded from the
Arabian Gulf, but identification needs verification. The
Indo-Pacific distribution is unclear; it is a common Australian species. Grey body mottled with brown. Clear fins.
    Lethrinus kallopterus Bleeker: Silvery body and orange
fins.
    Lethrinus miniatus (Bloch and Schneider): Recorded
from the Arabian Gulf. Red margin on fins.

yellowish

Pale blue.   L. MINIATUS

Darker yellow.
Pale yellow.

89

Family SPARIDAE

Porgies, or sea bream, are found in all temperate and tropical seas. A few species enter fresh-water. These carnivorous fishes eat crustaceans and molluscs, and are excellent food fishes. Some species are hermaphroditic. Characterised by molar-like teeth, large scales, scales on the preoperculum, and a single, continuous dorsal fin. The second anal fin spine is much longer than the first. Most species are silvery to pink. There are about ten common inshore species of porgies in the Arabian Gulf.

Acanthopagrus berda (Forskål)   Dark-finned porgy
Throughout Arabian Gulf; Africa to Australia, Polynesia.
    A fish found more often offshore, and on coral reefs. An elongate fish with long pectoral fins. Body darker than that of *A. latus*. Fins are clear to grey. Length: 75 cms.

Acanthopagrus bifasciatus (Forskål)
                              Two-banded porgy (Plate V)
Throughout Arabian Gulf; Africa to East Indies.
    A common and conspicuous fish around rock substrates in shallow water and on coral reefs. Distinguished by two vertical, black bands on the head, one through the eye from the top of the head to the angle of the jaw, and the other from the top of the head along the edge of the operculum. The fins, except for the pectoral fins, have black margins. Dorsal, caudal and pectoral fins are yellow. Body silvery. Incisor-like teeth are found towards the front of the mouth, and molar-like teeth towards the back. Length: 50 cms.

Acanthopagrus cuvieri (Day)   Black porgy
Throughout Arabian Gulf; Arabian Gulf, Arabian Sea, Indian Ocean.
    Similar to *A. berda*, but can be distinguished in that its molar-like teeth are in two or three rows as opposed to four or five rows as in *A. berda*. In addition, there is no notch

between the spinous and soft dorsal fins as in *A. berda*.
Length: 35 cms.

Acanthopagrus latus (Houttuyn) Yellow-finned porgy
Throughout Arabian Gulf; Arabian Gulf to Japan.
  A common species over both sand and rock substrates.
Frequents estuaries as a juvenile. Similar to *A. bifasciatus*,
but lacks the black bands on the head and black margins on
fins. The fins are yellow, body silvery. This species is a
protandrous hermaphrodite (male early in life; becomes
female later). Length: 45 cms.

Argyrops filamentosus (Valenciennes)
                                        Red-striped sea bream
= *Sparus filamentosus* (Valenciennes)
  Throughout Arabian Gulf; Africa to India.
  First dorsal spine elongated. The members of this genus
are deeper-bodied than species of *Acanthopagrus*. Length:
35 cms.

Argyrops spinifer (Forskål) Long-finned sea bream
Throughout Arabian Gulf; Africa to East Indies, Australia.
  A very common Gulf porgy, especially around coral
reefs. The first five dorsal spines bear elongate filaments in
adults; the first eight in juveniles. Adult males may develop
a hump in front of the dorsal fin. Body pinkish. Length:
60 cms.

Cheimerius nufar (Valenciennes) Barred sea bream
Throughout Arabian Gulf; Arabian Gulf to Africa.
  Probably an uncommon Gulf species, and from deeper,
offshore waters. Six vertical bars on body, the first through
the eye. Length: 60 cms.

Crenidens crenidens (Forskål) sea bream
Throughout Arabian Gulf; Indian Ocean.
  A common Gulf species which is found inshore as

juveniles. Distinguished by equally convex (rounded out-ward) dorsal and ventral contours. Dorsal and caudal fins bear a dark margin, and body and fins are generally olive-grey. There are 55–65 lateral line scales. Length: 30 cms.

Diplodus noct (Valenciennes)
One-spot sea bream (Plate VI)
Throughout Arabian Gulf; Indian Ocean.

This species is perhaps the most common inshore porgy, and one of the most common species of fish around rock substrates in the Arabian Gulf. Easily identified by a conspicuous black spot on the caudal peduncle. *Diplodus noct* may be a synonym of *D. sargus* (Linnaeus). Length: 30 cms.

Rhabdosargus sarba (Forskål)   Silver bream
Status in the Arabian Gulf unclear; East Africa, Red Sea to Australia, Japan.

Bright yellow abdomen. Yellow stripe on head. Length: 45 cms.

Family SCIAENIDAE

Drums are commercially important fishes of all temperate and tropical seas. Although mostly coastal marine in distribution, many species enter estuaries, especially as juveniles, and a few enter fresh water. They are called drums, or croakers, because of the croaking sounds which they produce by rubbing muscles against the air bladder wall and by regulating contraction and expansion of the air bladder. Carnivores which eat fish, crustaceans, and molluscs. Produce pelagic eggs. Spinous and soft dorsal fins are nearly separate, and the anal fin has either one or two spines. Tail rounded, squared or pointed. Mouth moderate to large, and small canine teeth are present in some species. Some have barbels on the chin. There are about eight common inshore drums in the Arabian Gulf, but the taxonomy of sciaenids in the Gulf requires much more study.

92

Johnius aeneus Bloch   Grey-finned croaker
= *Pseudosciaena aeneus* (Bloch)
   Throughout Arabian Gulf; Indian Ocean.
   A frequently encountered croaker. Body silvery. Fins
yellow with a grey edge. Caudal fin truncate to rounded.
Length: 25 cms.

Johnius maculatus Bloch and Schneider   Spotted drum
Recorded from the southern Arabian Gulf, but probably
occurs throughout; Arabian Gulf to East Indies.
   A lesser-known species than other *Johnius* and *Otolithes*.
Identifiable by the presence of large dark blotches on the
body. Otherwise resembles *J. aeneus*. Length: 45 cms.

Otolithes argenteus Valenciennes   Silver drum
Throughout Arabian Gulf; Arabian Gulf to Australia,
Melanesia.
   A common, commercially important species found in
shallow water. Silvery with a dark blotch on the oper-
culum. The spinous dorsal fin is dark. Length: 75 cms.

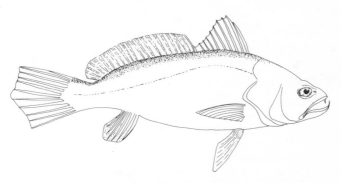

Fig. 24 *Otolithes ruber*

Otolithes ruber (Bloch and Schneider)
                                Red drum (Fig. 24)
Throughout Arabian Gulf; Africa to East Indies.
   A shallow-water fish caught by fishermen in large num-
bers on hand lines and in traps and seines. Fishes of this

genus are characterised by the large canine teeth in the jaws. The Red drum can be distinguished from *O. argenteus* by its generally darker colour (red-brown), and the lack of a blotch on the operculum. It is probable that this fish has not been clearly distinguished from *O. argenteus* in many references to Arabian Gulf fishes. Length: 1 m.

Pseudosciaena axillaris (Valenciennes)   drum
Throughout Arabian Gulf; Arabian Gulf to East Indies.
   Common. Outer portion of first dorsal fin dark. Length: 25 cms.

Pseudosciaena carutta (Bloch)   Banded drum
Southern Arabian Gulf; Arabian Gulf to Australia.
   Characterised by a pale lateral stripe that encloses the lateral line sensory pores, and a dark first dorsal fin.

Pseudosciaena diacanthus (Lacépède)   drum
Recorded from Strait of Hormuz and probably occurs in the Arabian Gulf; Arabian Gulf to Australia, East Indies.
   Black dots on the yellow fins and body. Length: 1·5 m.

Sciaena dussumieri (Valenciennes)   Bearded drum
Recorded from the southern Arabian Gulf; Africa to Melanesia.
   Single barbel at the midline of the lower jaw. Body coloration copper-brown. Length: 25 cms.

Family MULLIDAE

Goatfishes are small, bottom-feeding fishes of the Atlantic and Indo-Pacific oceans. Carnivorous fishes which obtain small crustaceans and annelid worms for food by probing into the sand or mud on the bottom. Found in shallow waters, usually over sand. Good food fishes. Characterised by two elongate chin barbels. The two dorsal fins are widely separated. Five species have been recorded from the Arabian Gulf, and it is likely that others will be found.

Mulloidichthys auriflamma (Forskål)
Golden-striped goatfish
Throughout Arabian Gulf; Indo-Pacific.
This common species of goatfish can be identified by the conspicuous golden-yellow stripe on the sides. Length: 40 cms.

Parapeneus pleurostigma (Bennett)   goatfish
Throughout Arabian Gulf; Indo-Pacific.
Rosy-coloured fish with a darker red spot behind the pectoral fins. Length: 30 cms.

Upeneus sulphureus Valenciennes   Yellow goatfish
Recorded only from Iraq, but probably occurs throughout the Arabian Gulf; Indo-Pacific.
Similar to *U. tragula* and *U. vittatus*, but the tail is not banded. Length: 30 cms.

Upeneus tragula Richardson
Black-striped goatfish (Plate VI)
Throughout Arabian Gulf; Africa to Japan.
The most generally encountered goatfish in the Arabian Gulf in shallow water. Frequents sandy substrates and patches of rock rubble, and can usually be seen in schools of five or six individuals. Easily distinguished from the similar *U. vittatus* by the conspicuous dark lateral stripe and small dark spots on the head and body. Length: 35 cms.

Upeneus vittatus (Forskål)   Bar-tailed goatfish
Throughout Arabian Gulf; Indo-Pacific.
Seemingly less common than *U. tragula*. Can be distinguished from that species by its lack of a lateral stripe and spots on body, and by its more prominent bars in the dorsal fins. Length: 30 cms.

95

Family MONODACTYLIDAE

Moonfishes are inhabitants of coastal marine and brackish waters, and sometimes coral reefs, throughout the Indo-Pacific region. Form schools. Used as aquarium fishes. Spawn in pairs and attach eggs to submerged objects. Deep-bodied, laterally compressed fishes with long dorsal and anal fin bases. Silvery. One species in the Arabian Gulf.

Monodactylus argenteus (Linnaeus)   Moonfish
Known only from the southern Arabian Gulf; Indo-Pacific.
    Silver with a vertical black stripe through the eye and a similar stripe from just in front of the dorsal fin, across the base of the pectoral fin, to the front of the anal fin. Length: 20 cms.

Family EPHIPPIDAE

Spadefishes are deep-bodied tropical and sub-tropical species of the Atlantic and Indo-Pacific oceans. Inhabitants of bays, estuaries, reefs and grass beds. Carnivorous. Edible, and often seen in markets. Produce pelagic eggs. Characterised by the presence of three anal spines, and separated spinous and soft dorsal fins. Small mouth. Two Arabian Gulf species.

Ephippus orbis (Bloch and Schneider)   spadefish
Throughout Arabian Gulf; Africa to Japan.
    Common, especially in more offshore waters, but entering bays and shallow coastlines. The third to fifth dorsal spines are extended as filaments. Body uniform golden colour. Length: 30 cms.

Drepane punctata (Linnaeus)   spadefish (Fig. 25)
= *Drepane longimana* (Bloch and Schneider)
    Throughout Arabian Gulf; Africa to East Indies.
    Common in both coastal and estuarine areas. Silver with

96

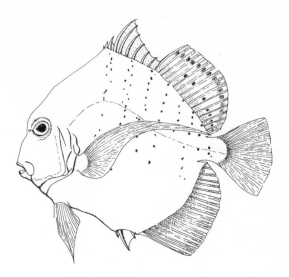

Fig. 25 *Orepane punctata*

four to eleven vertical rows of spots, or complete vertical bars, on sides. Sickle-shaped pectoral fins. Length: 45 cms.

Family PLATACIDAE

Batfishes, close relatives of the spadefishes (Ephippidae), and often classified with that family, are tropical Indo-Pacific species of both bay and reef habitats. Scavengers. Edible. Popular aquarium fishes. Young fish have very high dorsal and anal fins, so much so that these fish are much taller than they are long. Adults become much rounder and have less tall vertical fins. The spinous and ray portions of the dorsal and anal fins are not separated. Three anal spines. Young may look like floating leaves. Dark-coloured, often with a red line from the snout to the front edge of the dorsal fin. Probably only one species in the Arabian Gulf.

97

Fig. 26 *Platax pinnatus*

Platax pinnatus (Linnaeus)   batfish (Fig. 26)
Known from Saudi Arabia and the UAE; Indo-Pacific.
   Known by several other names, notably *P. teira* and
P. orbicularis. These are probably synonyms although
taxonomists disagree on this point. Length: 65 cms.

Family SCATOPHAGIDAE

Scats are deep-bodied fishes related to spadefishes, batfishes, and butterflyfishes. They are Indo-Pacific species
which inhabit estuaries, bays and coral reefs. Feed on
decaying matter and excrement, but despite these ob-
noxious habits are good to eat. Young individuals are kept
as aquarium pets. The spinous and ray portions of the
dorsal fin are continuous, but nearly separated by a deep
notch. Four anal spines. One species found in the Arabian
Gulf.

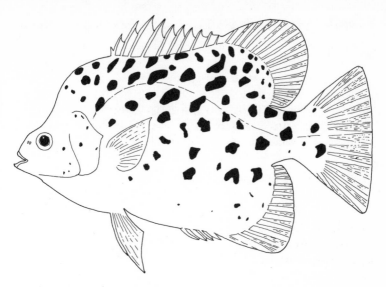

Fig. 27 *Scatophagus argus*

Scatophagus argus (Linnaeus)   Spotted scat (Fig. 27)
Throughout Arabian Gulf; Indian Ocean to Japan, Australia.

Inhabits bays, harbours, estuaries and coral reefs. Light green colour with black spots all over. Young have dark vertical bands and are red on the back and head. Length: 30 cms.

Family CHAETODONTIDAE

Butterflyfishes and angelfishes are diverse, tropical, coral reef-dwelling fishes. Eat small invertebrates. Generally not used as food fish. Deep-bodied, beautifully coloured fishes which are prized aquarium pets. Mouth small and teeth comb-like. The snout of some species is prolonged for reaching into crevices on coral reefs for food. Scales are rough (ctenoid) and dorsal, anal and caudal fins are scaled. Six species are known from the Arabian Gulf, but coral reefs in the southern Gulf should be expected to harbour additional species.

Chaetodon malapterus Guichenot   butterflyfish
Recorded from Saudi Arabia, but probably more wide-spread; Arabian Gulf and northern Arabian Sea.

Inhabits coral reefs. Yellow body and black tail. Soft dorsal and anal fins dark. Snout black. Length: 12 cms.

Chaetodon obscurus Boulenger
                         Dark butterflyfish (Plate VI)
Throughout Arabian Gulf; restricted to Arabian Gulf and southern Arabian Peninsula.

The most common Gulf butterflyfish. *Chaetodon nigropunctatus* Sauvage, from Muscat, is probably a synonym. Inhabits coral reefs, but may be expected to occur in any rocky, shallow water. Body and fins chocolate-brown, caudal fin with a yellow edge, and snout white. Length: 12 cms.

Heniochus acuminatus (Linnaeus)
                         Pennant butterflyfish (Plate VI)
Throughout Arabian Gulf; Africa to Japan, Hawaii.

A beautiful butterflyfish found on coral reefs. Fourth spine of dorsal fin extended as a long white filament. Pectoral fin, posterior part of dorsal fin, and caudal fin are all yellow. Eyes connected by a black bar. Two black bars, one from the dorsal fin to the pelvic fins, and another from the dorsal fin to the anal fin. Body otherwise white. Length: 25 cms.

Pomacanthus imperator (Bloch)   Imperial angelfish
Throughout Arabian Gulf; Indo-Pacific.

Coral reef inhabitant. A beautiful fish with yellow longitudinal lines on a grey-brown background which extend from behind the head over the body and on to the dorsal fin and caudal peduncle. The eyes are masked by a bar. Young are blue with semi-circular light markings on the body, dorsal fin and anal fin. Length: 40 cms.

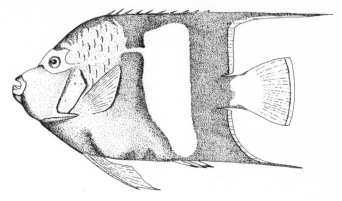

Fig. 28 *Pomacanthus maculosus*

Pomacanthus maculosus (Forskål)
                    Yellow-marked angelfish (Fig. 28)
Throughout Arabian Gulf; Arabian Gulf, Red Sea and western Indian Ocean.

Inhabits coral reefs. Usually encountered in pairs or threes. Blue-grey in colour with a wide yellow band from the dorsal fin to the area over the middle of the anal fin. Confused with *Arusetta asfur* (Forskål) which has also been recorded from the Arabian Gulf. In this latter species the wide yellow band on the body is in front of the anal fin; the occurrence of *A. asfur* in the Gulf should be verified. Length: 30 cms.

Pygoplites diacanthus (Boddaert)   angelfish
Recorded from Saudi Arabia; Indo-Pacific.

Yellow-orange with about nine blue-bordered white vertical bars. Dorsal and anal fins blue. Length: 20 cms.

101

Family POMACENTRIDAE

Damselfishes are small coral reef-dwelling fishes of both the Atlantic and Indo-Pacific oceans. Many inhabit rocky areas and jetties. Carnivores. Considered to be good food fish, but small. Attach adhesive eggs to submerged objects: some parental care is known, especially in the genus *Amphiprion*. There is a single pair of nostrils, as opposed to the two pairs of most fishes. Scales are large and rough, covering both head and body, and sometimes the dorsal, anal and caudal fins. The dorsal fin is long, the caudal fin deeply forked. Three species are known from the Arabian Gulf, but additional species should be expected on coral reefs in the southern Gulf, especially of the genera *Amphiprion* and *Abudefduf*.

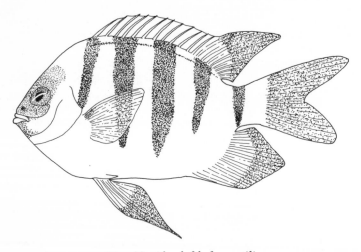

Fig. 29 *Abudefduf saxatilis*

Abudefduf saxatilis (Linnaeus) Sergeant major (Fig. 29)
Throughout Arabian Gulf; circumtropical.
Widespread on both Pacific and Atlantic coral reefs, and

102

more likely to be found on temperate rocky substrates (e.g. jetties) than most damselfishes. May be found mixed in with schools of *Pristotis jerdoni*. Preopercular margin smooth. Body yellow with five distinct vertical bars. Length: 18 cms.

Amphiprion clarkii (Bennett)   Clark's clownfish
Known from Saudi Arabia, but surely occurs on coral reefs elsewhere in the southern Arabian Gulf; Arabian Gulf to Japan.

The *Amphiprion* damselfishes (or clownfishes) enter into a symbiotic relationship with sea anemones of the genus *Stoichactis* on coral reefs. They nestle into the tentacles of the sea anemone and thereby gain protection. They appear either to anaesthetise the stinging cells of the tentacles, or they develop a tolerance to being stung. As a result of their attractive colour and unusual habits the clownfishes are popular aquarium pets. Of more than 25 Indo-Pacific species, only *A. clarkii* is known with certainty to occur in the Arabian Gulf. It is a brown fish with a broad white vertical bar through the eye, and another such bar below the middle of the dorsal fin. Resembles *A. sebae* of the southern Arabian coast, but which has not been recorded from the Gulf. Length: 15 cms.

Pristotis jerdoni (Day)   Jerdon's damelfish (Plate VII)
= *Daya jerdoni* (Day), and *Pomacentrus sindensis* (Day)
One of the most abundant fishes in the Arabian Gulf, Jerdon's damselfish, or Violet damselfish, reaches its greatest abundance on coral reefs, where it forms schools of hundreds of individuals. It can also be found over most rocky substrates. The spinous portions of the dorsal and anal fins lack scales, but there is a scaly sheath at the base of these fins. Preopercle bone serrated. Further characterised by a black dot above the axil of the pectoral fin. Most body scales have a blue centre. Body coloration is light blue and the tail is faint yellow. Length: 15 cms.

Family MUGILIDAE

Mullet are found in all tropical and sub-tropical seas, and are common estuarine fishes. Bottom-feeders, they ingest the mud or sand substrate along with small invertebrates and algae. All species are excellent, easily caught food fishes. Characterised by two widely separated dorsal fins, the first with four spines. Teeth are small or absent. Colour is silver. Three common species in inshore waters of the Arabian Gulf.

Mugil dussumieri (Cuvier and Valenciennes)
Brown-banded mullet
Throughout Arabian Gulf; Arabian Gulf to Australia, China.
Characterised by 28–32 lateral line scales and five longitudinal stripes on the sides. Length: 35 cms.

Mugil macrolepis (Smith)
Large-scaled mullet (Plate VII)
Throughout Arabian Gulf; Africa to Japan, Melanesia.
Perhaps the most common species of mullet in the Arabian Gulf. Has 31–35 scales in the lateral line, and dark margins on the dorsal and caudal fins. Length: 35 cms.

Mugil seheli (Forskål)
Blue-tailed, Long-finned, or Sand mullet
Throughout Arabian Gulf; Africa to Pacific Islands.
Common. Can be distinguished by the high number of lateral line scales (38–42), and the prominent spot at the base of the pectoral fin. Length: 50 cms.

Other species recorded from the Arabian Gulf (should be verified)
Mugil vaigensis Quoy and Gaimard: Diamond-scaled mullet. Length: 60 cms.
Mugil cephalus Linneaus: Sea mullet. A wide-ranging species which probably occurs in the Gulf. Length: 50 cms.

Mugil diadema Gilchrist and Thompson: Basket mullet.
Length: 75 cms.

Family SPHYRAENIDAE

Barracudas are large, fast-swimming, voracious, predatory
fishes of all tropical and sub-tropical seas. Edible, but large
specimens are a source of the dangerous ciguatera poison-
ing and should not be consumed. Spawn offshore and
produce pelagic eggs. Elongate, silvery fishes with large
canine teeth and strong jaws. Two widely separated dorsal
fins. Scales are small and the tail is forked. There are three
common species recorded from the Arabian Gulf.

Sphyraena flavicauda (Rüppell)   Dingofish
Known from the UAE; Africa to Melanesia.
   Yellow fins and one or two stripes on body. How accu-
rately this species has been distinguished from *S. jello* and
S. obtusata in references to Arabian Gulf fishes is unclear.
Length: 40 cms.

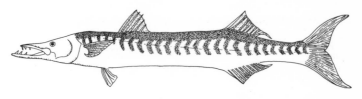

Fig. 30 *Sphyraena jello*

Sphyraena jello Cuvier and Valenciennes
                              Slender sea-pike (Fig. 30)
Throughout Arabian Gulf; Africa to Polynesia
   A very common Arabian Gulf species, often seen in
small schools near coral reefs or rocky areas. Easily recognised by 10–14 vertical bars on the body between the
pectoral fins and caudal peduncle. Angle of the preoperculum rounded. Potentially dangerous. Length: 2 m.

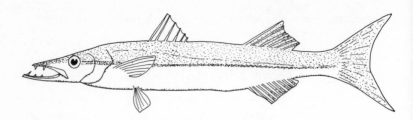

Fig. 31 *Sphyraena obtusata*

Sphyraena obtusata (Cuvier and Valenciennes)
Striped sea-pike (Fig. 31)
Throughout Arabian Gulf; Africa to Polynesia.

Inhabits grass beds and sandy areas, often in very shallow water. Has a distinct lateral stripe (olive to yellow in colour) from the snout through the eye to the caudal fin base. The lateral line is just above this stripe, and angles away from the stripe toward the head. Angle of preoperculum squared. Length: 50 cms.

Other species
Sphyraena japonica Schlegel: Recorded tentatively from the Arabian Gulf, but its occurrence there should be verified, as it has been perhaps confused with *S. jello*. Green with 12 dark cross-bars. Length: 1·8 m.

Family POLYNEMIDAE

Threadfins are marine, coastal species of tropical and subtropical areas. Carnivorous. Excellent food fish. Produce pelagic eggs, and some species enter estuaries to spawn. Easily identified by four to seven detached fin rays on the ventral side of the pectoral fins. Other characteristics include a large sub-terminal mouth, two widely separated dorsal fins, and a deeply forked caudal fin. There are two common inshore species in the Arabian Gulf.

106

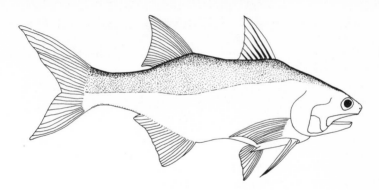

Fig. 32 *Eleutheronema tetradactylum*

Eleutheronema tetradactylum (Shaw)
                                    Giant threadfin (Fig. 32)
Throughout Arabian Gulf; Arabian Gulf to East Indies.
   Very common, slender, silvery fish with yellow pectoral
and anal fins. Four detached pectoral fin rays. Forms large
schools. Length: 1·8 m.

Polydactylus sextarius (Bloch and Schneider)
                              Six-threaded threadfin (Plate VII)
Throughout Arabian Gulf; Africa to Melanesia.
   Resembles *Eleutheronema tetradactylum*, but with six
detached pectoral fin rays, and a black spot at the beginning of the lateral line. Length: 30 cms.

Family LABRIDAE

Wrasses are common inhabitants of rock substrates,
especially coral reefs, throughout the tropical and sub-
tropical waters of the world. All species are marine. Diur-
nally active fishes which sleep at night in crevices or buried
in sand. Exhibit a wide variety of feeding habits ranging
from herbivore to carnivore, and some species are cleaners
which remove parasites from the body surface and gills of

107

other fishes. Elongate fish with smooth scales. Teeth are numerous, small and conical in shape, although canine teeth may be present in some species. There is a single, long dorsal fin. Colour patterns are variable and differ with age and sex. Change of sex from female to male is known in some species. The number of species in the Arabian Gulf is not known with certainty.

Choerodon robustus (Günther)   Tuskfish
Throughout Arabian Gulf; Africa to Australia.

Uncommon, especially inshore in the northern Gulf. Large head and outward directed canine teeth. Length: 30 cms.

Halichoeres hyrtli (Bleeker)   wrasse
Throughout Arabian Gulf; Arabian Gulf to China.

This is perhaps the most common wrasse species in the Arabian Gulf, and is found along shorelines in rock rubble and on coral reefs. Considerable confusion exists as to the true identity of this species. In the Arabian Gulf this species may well prove to be a species distinct from the widespread *H. hyrtli*, but this remains to be determined. Kuronuma & Abe (1972), in their book on Kuwait fishes, listed this species from Kuwait as *Stethojulis interrupta* (Bleeker), a species which is not known with certainty from the Gulf. *Halichoeres hyrtli* can be recognised by the black spot at the base of the pectoral fin. Length: 12 cms.

Labroides dimidiatus (Cuvier and Valenciennes)
                              Cleaner wrasse
Recorded from Saudi Arabia and the UAE, but may be expected on coral reefs throughout the Arabian Gulf; Indo-Pacific.

Easily recognised by the broad, black band from the snout, through the eye, and onto the body and tail. The black band is bordered with blue. The Cleaner wrasse removes parasites and debris from the skin and gills of a variety of other fishes. Length: 10 cms.

Pseudojulis trifasciatus Weber   wrasse
Occurrence in the Arabian Gulf tentative; Indo-Pacific.

This species has been recorded from the Arabian Gulf by Kuronuma & Abe (1972), but since their specimens actually came from the Gulf of Oman, the existence of *P. trifasciatus* in the Arabian Gulf remains to be proved. A distinct dark spot on the side is an aid to identification. Length: 10 cms.

Thalassoma lunare (Linnaeus)   Moon wrasse
Throughout Arabian Gulf; Indian Ocean.

Frequents rocky areas and coral reefs. The lunate tail and blue-bordered pectoral fins make this an easily identified fish. Length: 30 cms.

Family SCARIDAE

Parrotfishes occur on coral reefs in all tropical seas. Little is known about the Arabian Gulf species. They seem to be rare in the northern Gulf, and more common on the coral reefs and grass beds of the southern Gulf. They browse on coral and sea grasses. Small schools are formed during the day. At night parrotfishes make mucus cocoons in which they sleep. Little is known of reproductive habits, but pelagic eggs are produced. Parrotfishes are distinguished by their bright, variable colour patterns; males, females, and juveniles of the same species may all have different coloration. Teeth are fused to form a parrot-like beak, a feature which provides easy recognition. Scales are smooth and very large. The number of Arabian Gulf species is uncertain, but five have been recorded and others should be expected. Identification is difficult due to variable colour patterns.

Scarus enneacanthus Lacépède   parrotfish
Southern Arabian Gulf; western Indian Ocean.

Body blue. Dorsal and anal fins edged with white. Pectoral fins blue. Four scales before the dorsal fin (predorsal scales). Length: 40 cms.

Scarus ghobban Forskål   parrotfish
= *Scarus guttatus* Bloch and Schneider, and *Scarus dussumieri* Valenciennes
   Southern Arabian Gulf; Indo-Pacific.
   Body orange to yellow. Centre of scales with blue spots, forming vertical bars on sides. Dorsal and anal fins orange with blue edges. Rim of upper lip orange and rim of lower lip green. Five or six scales before the dorsal fin. Length: 50 cms.

Scarus janthochir Bleeker   parrotfish
Recorded from the Arabian Gulf; Africa to Pacific Islands.
   Body green or blue-green. Dorsal portion of head red. Teeth green. Snout and throat green. Caudal, pelvic and anal fins green with red markings. The dorsal and anal fins have blue edges. Six predorsal scales. Length: 50 cms.

Scarus oviceps Valenciennes   parrotfish
Southern Arabian Gulf; Indo-Pacific.
   Females have two or three yellow bars, or saddles, that slant up and back on the body. Males lack such bars but can be distinguished by a blue line from the snout under the eye to the operculum, thus separating a dark dorsal region from a more yellow ventral region. Six or seven predorsal scales. Length: 45 cms.

Scarus sordidus Forskål   parrotfish
Recorded from the UAE; Africa to Hawaii.
   Green body colour becoming pink ventrally. Dark spots on body scales. Dorsal and anal fins with a blue edge. Teeth white in young and becoming green in adults. Four predorsal scales. Length: 90 cms.

Family PARAPERCIDAE

Grubfishes, or weeverfishes, are bottom-dwelling marine species of the Indo-Pacific region and South Atlantic. Carnivorous. Found in grass beds and among rock rubble.

110

Edible. The first dorsal fin is vertically and longitudinally shorter than the second dorsal fin, and is connected to it by a membrane. Dorsal fin spines are sharp and can inflict a painful sting. The mouth is large and the eyes are positioned dorsally. Two species, found in both deep and shallow water, are definitely known from the Arabian Gulf.

Parapercis cylindrica (Bloch)   grubfish
= *P. hexopthalmus* Valenciennes
   Throughout Arabian Gulf; Red Sea to East Indies.
   This species has probably been recorded from the Arabian Gulf as *P. smithii* (Regan) by earlier workers, and has possibly been listed under *P. nebulosus* as well. It is recognised by the large black blotch in the tail and vertical bars, formed by dark-edged scales, on the body. Scales on the cheeks are large. Length: 30 cms.

Parapercis nebulosus (Quoy and Gaimard)
                              grubfish, or Bar-faced weeverfish
Throughout Arabian Gulf; Africa to East Indies.
   Common inhabitant of grass beds and rock rubble areas. Territorial, aggressive and conspicuous. The first dorsal fin is black and there are seven or eight saddle markings on the back. Three blue lines connect the eye and upper lip, and there is a curved blue line over the snout. Cheek scales are small. General coloration is reddish dorsally and a lighter, cream colour ventrally. Fins tend to be pink. Outer caudal fin rays may be extended as filaments in adults. Length: 30 cms.

Family BLENNIIDAE

Blennies constitute a large and diverse group of essentially marine fishes. Primarily tropical, but found in temperate seas as well, they inhabit rocky shorelines, coral reefs, and estuaries. Carnivorous. Mostly small species and of no value as food fishes. Eggs are attached to shells or rocks and are guarded by the parents. Scales are usually absent.

111

The dorsal fin is long, and pelvic fins are far forward on the body, in front of the pectoral fins. Mouth large, often with canine teeth. Tentacles may be present on the head. These fishes are poorly known in the Arabian Gulf and identifications are difficult. About eight shallow-water species are definitely known from the Gulf, and additional species are certain to be recorded.

Antennablennius persicus (Regan)   blenny
= *Blennius persicus* Regan
     Known only from the southern Arabian Gulf.
     Found in tide-pools. No canine teeth. First dorsal fin with three broad stripes. Length: 5 cms.

Fig. 33 *Ecsenius pulcher*

Ecsenius pulcher (Murray)   Pretty blenny (Fig. 33)
Known from Kuwait and Saudi Arabia, but probably occurs throughout Arabian Gulf; Arabian Sea.
     Inhabits rock rubble and coral reefs. Two colour phases: (a) uniform brown, and (b) brown anteriorly with five to eight blue, vertical bars on an unpigmented area on the rear half of the body. Length: 6 cms.

Istiblennius lineatus (Valenciennes)   blenny
Recorded from the southern Arabian Gulf; Arabian Gulf to East Indies.
     Tide-pools. No canine teeth. Males have a crest on the head. There is a deep notch between the first and second dorsal fins. The second dorsal fin has oblique stripes which rise posteriorly. Length: 10 cms.

112

Omobranchus fasciolatus (Valenciennes)　　　blenny
Known from Kuwait and Saudi Arabia, but probably
occurs throughout the Arabian Gulf; Africa through
northern Arabian Sea.
　Tide-pools. Canine teeth present in upper jaw but not in
lower. Blade-like crest on top of head. Dark, round spot on
the soft dorsal fin. Length: 5 cms.

Omobranchus mekranensis Regan　　　blenny
Recorded from the Arabian Gulf, but exact locality unknown; northern Arabian Sea and Arabian Gulf.
　Habitat unknown. Canine teeth in upper jaw but not in
lower. Blade-like crest on head. No dark spot on the soft
dorsal fin (distinguishes this species from *O. fasciolatus*).
Length: 4 cms.

Omobranchus punctatus (Valenciennes)　Spotted blenny
Recorded from Iran (in northern Gulf) and Kuwait;
circumtropical distribution.
　Canine teeth present in upper jaw but not in lower. No
blade-like crest on head. Broad, dark band extending over
body in front of dorsal fin (may be represented by three
distinct blotches). Length: 7 cms.

Petroscirtes ancylodon (Rüppell)　　　blenny
Known from Kuwait and Saudi Arabia; Red Sea and
Arabian Gulf.
　Enlarged canine teeth in lower jaw. The first dorsal spine
is shorter than or equal to the fourth dorsal spine in length,
and is shorter than the second dorsal spine. May be found
in attached clumps of seaweeds in shallow water. Length:
9 cms.

Petroscirtes mitratus (Rüppell)　　　blenny
Known from Kuwait and Saudi Arabia; Africa to Australia, Polynesia.
　Enlarged canine teeth present in lower jaw. The first
dorsal spine is longer than the second and fourth dorsal

spines, a feature which will distinguish this species from *P. ancylodon*. Length: 9 cms.

Family GOBIIDAE

Gobies are a diverse group of fishes found in all seas, and occasionally in fresh water, from shallow shorelines to deeper waters, and in a variety of habitats ranging from mud flats to coral reefs. Most species are carnivorous with a large mouth, but some sift mud through comb-like teeth for invertebrates and algae. This is the largest fish family with about 800 species, and most species are poorly known. Many are small, secretive species found only in holes or crevices. Some symbiotically inhabit burrows of other animals such as crabs, shrimp or other fishes, or bodies of sponges. A few species are cleaners which remove parasites from bodies of other fishes. Eggs are usually placed in a cluster of shells or amongst plants, and are guarded. Some place eggs in holes in mud or in coral crevices. Gobies are distinguished by fused pelvic fins which form a ventral sucker, and two separated dorsal fins. Scales, if present, are usually small. Several species of goby are known from inshore waters of the Arabian Gulf, several more from offshore waters, and many more species should be expected.

Bathygobius fuscus (Rüppell)   goby (Plate VII)
Throughout Arabian Gulf; Indo-Pacific.
    A drab, brown-coloured goby of shallow, rocky areas and tide-pools. Poorly known. The ventral rays of the pelvic fin are free from the rest of the fin. Length: 12 cms.

Boleophthalmus boddarti (Pallas)

mudskipper (Plate VII)
Kuwait, Iraq, and Iran (northern Gulf only); Indian Ocean.
    A large mudskipper which is more amphibious than *Scartelaos viridis*, but which lives on the same mud flats in the northern Arabian Gulf. Not known from the southern

114

Gulf. A robust species. As in *S. viridis* the third spine of the first dorsal fin is elongated as a filament, but not so markedly as in *S. viridis*. The base of the first dorsal fin is as long as the fin is high (in *S. viridis* the first dorsal fin is higher than it is long). The second dorsal fin and anal fin are elongate, each with 25 or more fin rays. There are no chin barbels in this species. The fine, comb-like teeth distinguish *B. boddarti* from other mudskippers as well. The ventral sucker is round, not indented posteriorly. This mudskipper sifts mud through its teeth and strains edible filamentous algae and possibly invertebrates from it. *Boleophthalmus boddarti* has been recorded as *Pseudapocryptes dentatus* (Cuvier and Valenciennes) from Kuwait (by Kuronuma & Abe, 1972) and as *Boleophthalmus pectinirostris* Osbeck from Iraq. The existence of these latter species in the Arabian Gulf, while possible, must be confirmed. Length: 20 cms.

Cryptocentrus cryptocentrus Cuvier and Valenciennes
goby

Known from Kuwait and Saudi Arabia, but probably occurs throughout the Arabian Gulf; East Africa to Japan.

A poorly known but very common fish which may indeed represent a species distinct from the widespread *C. cryptocentrus*, but which for now should be allotted to that species. Lives in snapping shrimp (*Alpheus*) burrows in shallow water, especially in sparse grass beds, to a depth of about 5 m. Common wherever there is a grass bed with a sand substrate. This goby appears to act as a sentinel for the industrious shrimps, usually a male-female pair, which maintain the burrow. The goby is olive-green with cream-coloured bands, and the shrimp possesses a remarkably similar colour pattern. Length: 10 cms.

Gobiodon citrinus (Rüppell)   Coral goby

Recorded from Saudi Arabia, but probably more widespread in the Arabian Gulf; East Africa to Melanesia.

A bright orange coral reef-dwelling goby. Length: 5 cms.

115

Periophthalmus koelreuteri (Pallas)

mudskipper (Plate VIII)

= *Periophthalmus waltoni* Koumans

Kuwait, Iraq, Iran (northern Gulf only); Africa to Melanesia.

The most amphibious of the Arabian Gulf mudskippers, *P. koelreuteri* is also known only from the mud flats of the northern Gulf. Like other mudskippers, it is active only during the day and at low tide. At night and during high tides mudskippers retreat into burrows. This species is an active predator of crustaceans, mainly fiddler crabs, and insects. *P. koelreuteri* routinely leaves the water and treks over drier land while hunting. It carries water in its gill and mouth cavities, and walks with its tail pointed upward, presumably to protect the delicate caudal fin membranes through which it is reported to breathe by placing the tail in the water while the rest of the body is exposed. It is easily distinguished from the other Arabian Gulf mudskippers by the enlarged canine teeth in both jaws (about 15 in both the upper and lower jaws), fleshy lips, very short second dorsal fin and anal fin, and rounded tail. The fused pelvic fins have a deep notch posteriorly, rather than being completely rounded into a sucker, a feature which distinguishes this species from *P. chrysospilos* Bleeker which has been erroneously recorded from the Arabian Gulf. *P. waltoni* Koumans is apparently a synonym of *P. keolreuteri*, and is a name that has been applied to specimens from Kuwait, Iraq, and Iran. Length: 15 cms.

Scartelaos viridis (Hamilton-Buchanan)

Bearded mudskipper (Plate VIII)

= *Scartelaos tenuis* (Day)

Kuwait, Iraq, Iran (northern Gulf only); Arabian Gulf to Australia.

A slender mudskipper which occurs in great numbers in the northern Arabian Gulf, but is not known from the southern Gulf. It lives in burrows on mud flats where it co-exists with the other two species of mudskippers listed

116

in this book. This amphibious fish is easily identified by the elongate third spine of the first dorsal fin. In addition, the first dorsal fin has a short base, the fin being much taller than the length of the fin base. The second dorsal fin and anal fin are very long, each with more than 25 rays. Other distinguishing features are the pointed caudal fin, the row of barbels on the chin, and two enlarged canine teeth toward the middle of the lower jaw. There are also about 15 canine teeth in the upper jaw. The ventral sucker is round. Like other mudskippers *S. viridis* is active only during daylight hours at low tide. This species is more aquatic than the other mudskippers of the Arabian Gulf. It is a predatory species. Length: 15 cms.

Family ACANTHURIDAE

Surgeonfishes are found in all tropical seas. Herbivorous. Occur on coral reefs and on grass beds. Known to produce pelagic eggs. Characterised by the presence of one or two retractable spines (scalpels) on the caudal peduncle. Deep-bodied fishes with small scales and a single, long dorsal fin. Three species are known from the Arabian Gulf, especially from the south, but additional species should be found with further study.

Acanthurus triostegus (Linnaeus)
Convict surgeonfish, or Five-banded surgeon (Fig. 34) Southern Arabian Gulf; Indo-Pacific.
Found on coral reefs and in rocky areas. Distinguished by five vertical bars on the body, the first one through the eye. Length: 25 cms.

Ctenochaetus striatus (Quoy and Gaimard)
Hairy-toothed tang
Reported from Iraq, and probably occurs throughout the Arabian Gulf; Indo-Pacific.
Coloration brown with wavy, longitudinal blue lines on sides. Known to spawn in groups on coral reefs in late

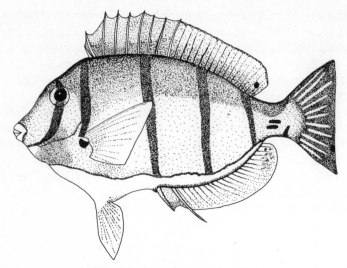

Fig. 34 *Acanthurus triostegus*

afternoon or near dusk; a correlation between spawning and the full moon has been suggested. Length: 18 cms.

Zebrasoma xanthurum (Blyth)   Sail-finned surgeonfish
Throughout Arabian Gulf; Africa to India.
   Inhabits coral reefs. Blue body and bright yellow tail. Length: 20 cms.

Other species
Acanthurus sohal (Forskål): Reported from Saudi Arabia, but the taxonomic status of this fish is unclear, and it may not be a valid species; perhaps confused with *Ctenochaetus striatus*. Has a dark body with wavy blue stripes. Inhabits coral reefs.

Family SIGANIDAE

The spine-feet, or rabbitfishes, are Indo-Pacific fishes. Herbivorous inhabitants of coral reefs and grass beds. Considered good to eat. Body laterally compressed, smooth, slimy. Has a long, continuous dorsal fin with very sharp, pointed spines which can inflict a painful sting. Three common species in the Arabian Gulf.

Siganus javus (Linnaeus)   spine-foot
Throughout Arabian Gulf; Africa to Australia.
   Distinguished from *S. oramin* by the combination of light spots anteriorly and light wavy lines on the posterior two-thirds of the body, and lack of a spot on the shoulder. Length: 30 cms.

Siganus oramin (Bloch and Schneider)
                    Pearl-spotted spine-foot (Plate VIII)
Throughout Arabian Gulf; Africa to Japan.
   The most common spine-foot in the Arabian Gulf. Pearl spots on the body provide easy recognition of this species. There is a dark, round spot on the shoulder. An inhabitant of grass beds. The pearl-spotted spine-foot is an important food fish. Length: 35 cms.

Siganus stellatus (Forskål)   Rabbitfish
Reported from the UAE; Indian Ocean.
   Occurrence of this species in the Arabian Gulf needs to be verified. Brown fish with black dots on body. Grass beds and rocky areas. Length: 45 cms.

Family TRICHIURIDAE

Elongate, silvery fishes of the Atlantic and Indo-Pacific region. Carnivorous. Edible. Body tapers to an elongated, pointed tail with no broad caudal fin. The dorsal fin extends from the head to the tip of the body. Pelvic fins are absent or very reduced. The mouth is large and has canine teeth. The snout is pointed. Probably only one species in the Arabian Gulf.

Trichiurus haumela (Forskål)   Cutlass fish (Fig. 35)
Throughout Arabian Gulf; Africa to Japan.

119

Fig. 35 *Trichiurus haumela*

This is probably the same species recorded as *T. muticus* (Gray) by other students of Arabian Gulf fishes. Often caught on hook and line, especially at night near jetties. Length: 1 m.

Family SCOMBRIDAE

Mackerels and tunas are pelagic marine fishes of all seas. They are fast-swimming, schooling predators encountered offshore. Characterised by very small scales, two well-separated dorsal fins, small finlets behind the second dorsal fin and anal fin, and a keel or keels on the caudal peduncle. Although several species may occur in the Arabian Gulf, only one is likely to be encountered in inshore waters.

Rastrelliger kanagurta (Cuvier) Golden-striped mackerel
Throughout Arabian Gulf; Indo-Pacific.
    Blue ·dorsally with irregular dark dots and mottling. Yellow band along the lateral line. Other characteristics in the family description. Length: 35 cms.

120

Order **PLEURONECTIFORMES**

Mostly marine. Both eyes on same side of head due to migration of one eye during development, resulting in an asymmetrical condition. Eyeless side turned toward the substrate. No pigment on the eyeless side and a reduction of the pectoral and pelvic fins on the eyeless side. Long dorsal and anal fins.

Key to Families of Pleuronectiformes in the Arabian Gulf

1. a. A spine present in the pelvic fins; pelvic fins symmetrical and not attached to the anal fin; mouth large .... Psettodidae (toothed flounders)

   b. No spines in pelvic fins; pelvic fins symmetrical or asymmetrical and may be joined to the anal fin; mouth large or small 2

2. a. Eyes on right side of body; mouth small .... Soleidae (soles)

   b. Eyes on left side of the body; mouth large or small 3

3. a. Dorsal and anal fins continuous with caudal fin; mouth small .... Cynoglossidae (tongue soles)

121

b. Dorsal and anal fins not
   continuous with caudal
   fin; mouth large or small   Bothidae
                                 (left-handed
                                 flounders)

Family PSETTODIDAE

The family Psettodidae is represented by a single species
in the Indo-Pacific region. Carnivorous. Edible. Characterised by a large mouth with sharp, pointed teeth. Eyes
either on the right or left side. Pelvic fins symmetrical.
Coloration as with most of the bottom-dwelling flatfish, is
brown.

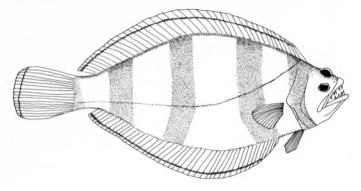

Fig. 36 *Psettodes erumei*

Psettodes erumei (Bloch and Schneider)

Halibut (Fig. 36)

Throughout Arabian Gulf; Africa to Australia, China.
   Found in shallow, coastal waters. A good food fish.
Length: 60 cms.

Family BOTHIDAE

Bothids are small flatfishes of shallow, coastal waters
throughout the temperate and tropical zones of the world.

122

Carnivorous. Good to eat. Eggs are known to be buoyant and float, but sink as development proceeds. Eyes on the left side, and the right pelvic fin is smaller than the left. Most species are brown or light brown with mottling. Of several species found in the Arabian Gulf, the following are likely to be encountered in inshore waters.

Arnoglossus aspilos (Bleeker)   flounder
Bahrain, UAE; Arabian Gulf to East Indies.
  This species is usually taken in shrimp trawls. Uniform brown in colour. Small, close-set teeth. Length: 10 cms.

Bothus pantherinus (Rüppell)   Leopard flounder
Throughout Arabian Gulf; Africa to Hawaii.
  The upper rays of the pectoral fin on the eyed side of the body are elongate, and provide an identifying characteristic. Pelvic fins are asymmetrical. Length: 30 cms.

Laeops guntheri Alcock   flounder
Throughout Arabian Gulf; Indian Ocean.
  Poorly known in the Arabian Gulf. Body brown with dark dorsal, anal, and caudal fins. Length: 15 cms.

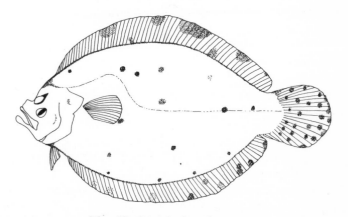

Fig. 37 *Pseudorhombus arsius*

123

Pseudorhombus arsius (Hamilton-Buchanan)
Large-toothed flounder (Fig. 37)
Throughout Arabian Gulf; Africa to Australia.

These flounders are perhaps the most common bothids in the Arabian Gulf. Jaws have enlarged canine teeth. The pigmented side of the body has numerous dusky blotches and one to three ocellated spots on the lateral line. A good food fish. Length: 30 cms.

Pseudorhombus elevatus Ogilby   Deep flounder
Throughout Arabian Gulf; Arabian Gulf to Australia.

This is a deeper water fish than *P. arsius*, and is less likely to be encountered, except in fish markets. Distinguished from *P. arsius* by the equal position of the eyes. In *P. arsius* the anterior margin of the right eye is slightly forward of the margin of the left eye. Length: 18 cms.

Pseudorhombus javanicus (Bleeker)   flounder
Throughout Arabian Gulf; Indian Ocean.

A poorly known species probably confused with *P. arsius* and *P. elevatus*. Eyes equal in position, and thus resembles *P. elevatus*. Differs from that species in that there is a distinct dark spot at the junction of the curved and straight portions of the lateral line. Found in grass beds. Length: 20 cms.

Family SOLEIDAE

Soles are primarily marine and estuarine species of all seas; a few species enter fresh water. Small predators. Good to eat. Produce pelagic eggs. Flatfishes with both eyes on the right side of the body. Pectoral fins are small, the right one being larger than the left. The dorsal and anal fins may or may not be fused to the caudal fin. Soles are bottom-dwelling species of shallow water, but are more likely to be caught by trawls than to be seen along a beach or while skin-diving. They may be caught on hook and line. At least five species may be found in the Arabian Gulf.

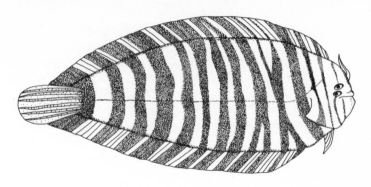

Fig. 38 *Aesopia cornuta*

Aesopia cornuta (Kaup)   Horned zebra sole (Fig. 38)
= *Synaptura cornuta* Kaup
　Throughout Arabian Gulf; Africa to Japan.
　An elongate sole of more offshore waters, this species
will be encountered mostly in fish markets. The first dorsal
fin ray, positioned in front of the eyes, is swollen. Dorsal
and anal fins are continuous with the caudal fin. Body
brown with 13–14 dark bands. Length: 20 cms.

Pardachirus marmoratus (Lacépède)
　　　　　　　　　　　　　　　　Spotted sole (Fig. 39)
Kuwait, Bahrain, and probably throughout Arabian Gulf;
Indian Ocean.
　Easily recognised by its light brown body with numerous
darker spots and blotches. Dorsal and anal fins are not
continuous with the caudal fin. Length: 25 cms.

Solea elongata Day   sole
Throughout Arabian Gulf; Indian Ocean.
　More elongate than *Pardachirus marmoratus*, but with a
similar colour pattern of a brown body with darker spots
and blotches. A distinguishing feature is a dark spot on the
outer half of the pectoral fin on the eyed side of the fish.
Length: 10 cms.

125

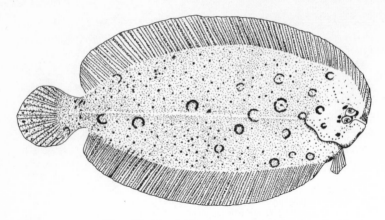

Fig. 39 *Pardachirus marmoratus*

Solea heinii Steindachner   sole
Known from two specimens from the Shatt-al-Arab estuary, Iraq.
  The status of this species in the Arabian Gulf needs to be investigated.

Synaptura orientalis (Bloch and Schneider)
                                    Black sole (Plate VIII)
= *Brachirus orientalis* (Bloch and Schneider)
  Throughout Arabian Gulf; Indo-Pacific.
  Elliptical-shaped sole in which the dorsal and anal fins are continuous with the caudal fin, such that the head and fins form a smooth, unbroken outline. Even the eyes and mouth may be difficult to discern. Dark olive-brown colour. Rough scales on both sides of body. Inhabits muddy embayments and estuaries. Length: 30 cms.

Family CYNOGLOSSIDAE

Tongue soles are elongate, left-eyed flounders of all seas and some freshwater circumstances. Small bottom-dwelling predators usually occurring in deep water. Good food fish. Dorsal and anal fins are continuous with the caudal fin, which tapers to a point. Pectoral fins are absent. Possibly three species in shallow waters of the Arabian Gulf; additional species in deeper water.

Cynoglossus arel (Schneider)   tongue sole
Throughout Arabian Gulf; Arabian Gulf to Taiwan.

Perhaps the most common tongue sole in the shallow waters of the Arabian Gulf. Most likely to be seen in fish markets. Has been recorded as *C. macrolepidotus* Bleeker from Kuwait by Kuronuma & Abe (1972), from the southern Gulf by White & Barwani (1971), and from Iran by Blegvad (1944). Menon (1977) calls this species *C. arel*. Scales are smooth on the blind side of the body. Length: 35 cms.

Cynoglossus bilineatus (Lacépède)   tongue sole
Recorded from the coast of Iran; Arabian Sea to East Indies, Australia.

The status of this species in the Arabian Gulf is unclear as Blegvad (1944) did not clearly distinguish this species from *C. arel* (as *C. macrolepidotus*). The most recent authority, Menon (1977), did not include the Arabian Gulf in the geographic range of *C. bilineatus*. Length: 35 cms.

Cynoglossus kopsi (Bleeker)   tongue sole
Known from the Arabian Gulf; Arabian Gulf to Indo-Australasian archipelago.

A wide-ranging species from deeper water and not likely to be encountered by readers of this book except in fish markets. Rough scales on the blind side. Length: 18 cms.

Order **TETRAODONTIFORMES**

Mostly marine. Operculum reduced and fleshy. Gill slit reduced, often only a small opening just in front of the pectoral fin. Pelvic fins reduced to a single spine or pair of spines, or completely absent. Scales reduced, modified into bony plates or absent. Often toxic if eaten.

Key to the Families of Tetraodontiformes in the Arabian Gulf

1. a. Pelvic fins reduced to a pair of stout spines .... Triacanthidae (triple-spines)

   b. Pelvic fins reduced to a single spine in the mid-line of the body, or absent   2

2. a. No dorsal fin spines   3
   b. One to three spines in the dorsal fin .... Balistidae (triggerfishes)

3. a. Well-developed spines all over the body .... Diodontidae (spiny puffers)

   b. No well-developed spines all over body; possibly small prickles present or body smooth   4

4. a. Body encased in bony armour (carapace) .... Ostraciodontidae (boxfishes)

   b. Body not encased in bony armour .... Tetraodontidae (puffers)

Family TRIACANTHIDAE

All but one species of triple-spine occur in the Indo-Pacific region. Predators. Generally not eaten. The most distinctive feature of these fishes is that the pelvic fins are reduced to a single stout spine in each fin, thereby giving a tripod appearance to the fish. Dorsal fins are well separated and the first dorsal spine is elongate. Scales are small and rough. The gill opening is a small slit in front of the pectoral fins. Two, possibly three, species in the Arabian Gulf.

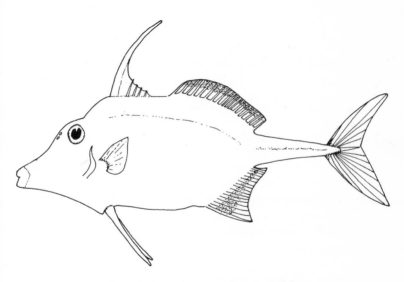

Fig. 40 *Pseudotriacanthus strigilifer*

Pseudotriacanthus strigilifer (Cantor)
                    Long-spined tripodfish (Fig. 40)
Throughout Arabian Gulf; Arabian Gulf to Melanesia.
    More common offshore. Elongate snout and yellow blotches on the sides of the body. The spinous dorsal fin is not black. Length: 18 cms.

Triacanthus biaculeatus (Bloch) Black-spined triple-spine
Throughout Arabian Gulf; Arabian Gulf to Melanesia.

A common species found in shallow water over sand substrates. The snout is short and the spinous dorsal fin is black. Length: 18 cms.

Triacanthus indicus Regan   triple-spine
Occurrence in the Arabian Gulf needs verification.

This species has been recorded from the Arabian Gulf but it has not been clearly delineated from *T. biaculeatus* which it resembles. It has a blackish spinous dorsal fin, as in *T. biaculeatus*, but is distinguished from that species by a black spot at the pectoral fin base.

Family BALISTIDAE

Triggerfishes and filefishes are marine species of all tropical and sub-tropical seas. Most species have poisonous flesh, but a few are edible. The triggerfishes (Balistinae) are usually colourful denizens of coral reefs, but are often found swimming far out to sea. There are herbivorous and carnivorous species. Leather-jackets, or filefishes (Monacanthinae) have one or two dorsal spines and triggerfishes (Balistinae) have three. The first dorsal spine has a locking mechanism so that it can be held rigidly erect. There are no pelvic fins, although a remnant spine may be present. Scales are small. Incisor-like teeth protrude from the upper jaw. At least six species occur in the inshore waters of the Arabian Gulf.

Abalistes stellaris (Bloch and Schneider)
                                  Starred triggerfish
Throughout Arabian Gulf, Africa to Melanesia, Australia.

Distinguished by a groove from the eye to the snout, narrow caudal peduncle, and concave caudal fin. Colour grey-green on back with small, light blue spots; lighter on abdomen. Considered to be edible. Length: 60 cms.

Paramonacanthus choirocephalus Bleeker
Pig-faced filefish
Throughout Arabian Gulf; Arabian Gulf and Arabian Sea to East Indies.

The front edge of the first dorsal spine is rough, and the rear edge has two rows of small barbs. The tail is round and the upper caudal fin rays may be extended as a filament. Large, moveable pelvic fin spine in the midline of the body. Length: 6 cms.

Paramonacanthus oblongus (Temminck and Schlegel)
Horse-faced filefish
Throughout Arabian Gulf; Arabian Gulf to Japan.

Resembles *P. choirocephalus* but can be distinguished from it by the smooth front edge of the first dorsal spine. In addition, the second dorsal fin ray is extended as a filament. Length: 16 cms.

Rhineacanthus aculeatus (Linnaeus)
White-barred triggerfish
Recorded only from Saudi Arabia, but may be expected to occur throughout the Arabian Gulf; Indo-Pacific.

Easily recognised by three rows of spines on the caudal peduncle. Length: 30 cms.

Stephanolepis diaspros Fraser-Brunner
Reticulated, or Freckled filefish
Recorded from Kuwait, Saudi Arabia and Bahrain, and probably occurs throughout the Arabian Gulf; Arabian Gulf to India and Sri Lanka.

The most common filefish and the one most likely to be encountered in the Arabian Gulf. Resembles *P. choirocephalus* and *P. oblongus*, but may be distinguished from them by the slightly curved (backward) dorsal spine, and by the triangular patch of spines on the caudal peduncle. Length: 20 cms.

Sufflamen capistratus (Shaw)   Masked triggerfish
Recorded from the southern Arabian Gulf, but probably
occurs throughout; Indo-Pacific.
   Distinguished by a yellow band from the lips to the
pectoral fins. Length: 50 cms.

Family OSTRACIODONTIDAE

Boxfishes, or trunkfishes, are marine fishes of the tropical
seas of the world. Most likely to be encountered on coral
reefs. Herbivorous. These are poisonous fishes which
should not be eaten. They can even be toxic to other fishes
in a confined aquarium by releasing toxins into the water.
Body enclosed in bony plates (a carapace), with only the
tail free. The fins are small and have no spines. Pelvic fins
are absent. Three species are known from the Arabian
Gulf.

Ostracion lentiginosum Bloch and Schneider   boxfish
Recorded only from the southern Gulf; Africa to Hawaii.
   Body colour brown to green with light blue spots. In-
habits coral reefs. Length: 20 cms.

Ostracion tuberculatus Linnaeus   boxfish
Recorded from Iraq and from the southern Arabian Gulf,
so should be expected to occur throughout; Indo-Pacific.
   Juveniles are bright yellow with black spots. Adults are
brown or green-brown with dark spots. These dark spots,
in turn, have blue centres. Fins are orange. Length: 45 cms.

Tetrosomus gibbosus (Linnaeus)   boxfish
= *Ostracion gibbosus* Linnaeus
   Throughout Arabian Gulf; Indo-Pacific.
   The most common boxfish in the Arabian Gulf. Distinguished by a sharp triangular spine on the back. Body
triangular in cross section. Each bony plate of the carapace
has a blue spot in the centre. There are strong spines on the
lateral ridges of the body. Length: 30 cms.

Family TETRAODONTIDAE

Puffers, or blowfishes, are found in all seas, although most species are tropical. A few species enter or live in estuaries or even fresh water. Some species form large schools, while others are more solitary inhabitants of grass beds and coral reefs. These fishes can inflate their bodies with either air or water. Predators. Most species are toxic to eat, but some can be a delicacy if specially prepared. Eggs are demersal (they sink) and adhere to submerged objects. In some species the males guard the eggs. There are no scales, but the body may be covered with small prickles. No spines in the fins. Pelvic fins are absent. Teeth in each jaw are fused to form a beak. Dorsal and anal fins are small. Four species of puffers occur inshore in the Arabian Gulf.

Arothron stellatus (Bloch and Schneider)   Starry puffer
Throughout Arabian Gulf; Africa to Australia, Melanesia.
    Body covered with small spines. Dorsal, anal and caudal fins rounded. Colour grey with numerous black spots on head, body and fins. The spots are smallest on the head and largest at the base of the pectoral fins. Length: 90 cms.

Chelonodon patoca (Hamilton-Buchanan)
                                                    Marbled puffer
Throughout Arabian Gulf; Africa to Australia, Melanesia.
    Small spines on back and on abdomen. Dorsal, anal and caudal fins rounded. Coloration brown with large green-white spots. Length: 35 cms.

Lagocephalus lunaris (Bloch and Schneider)
                                                    Green puffer
= *Gastrophysus lunaris* (Bloch and Schneider), and *Spheroides lunaris* (Bloch and Schneider)
    Throughout Arabian Gulf; Africa to Japan.
    Easily identified by dark green dorsal colour and yellow sides. The caudal peduncle is very narrow. Dorsal, anal and caudal fins are all sickle-shaped. Length: 30 cms.

133

Lagocephalus scleratus (Gmelin)   Silver-banded puffer
Throughout Arabian Gulf; Africa to Japan.
   Dorsal part of body grey-brown with dark spots. Ventral
half of body white. Dorsal, anal and caudal fins sickle-
shaped. Caudal peduncle very narrow. Length: 75 cms.

Family DIODONTIDAE

Porcupinefishes are marine, tropical fishes found on coral
reefs and in weedy areas. They can inflate their bodies with
air or water. They produce eggs which sink to the bottom
and adhere to the substrate. Pelvic fins are absent. Teeth
are fused into a parrot-like beak. Three species are known
from the Arabian Gulf.

Cyclichthys echinatus (Gray)   Fringed porcupinefish
Known from the southern Arabian Gulf; circumtropical
distribution.
   Spines on the body have three roots where the spine
attaches to the skin. Colour is brown with black spots on
the head and body. Length: 20 cms.

Cyclichthys orbicularis (Bloch)   Round porcupinefish
Known from the southern Arabian Gulf; circumtropical
distribution.
   Similar to *C. echinatus*, but with large spots found only
on the body, not on the head. Length: 20 cms.

Diodon hystrix Linnaeus   porcupinefish
Known from Saudi Arabia, but probably more widespread
in the Arabian Gulf; circumtropical distribution.
   Spines on the body have two roots. Length: 90 cms.

134

Bibliography

Al-Daham, Najim K. (1976). Fishes of Iraq and the Arab Gulf: Orders Squaliformes and Rajiformes. *Bulletin, Basrah Natural History Museum*, **3**: 3–52.

Allen, G. R. (1975). *Damselfishes of the South Seas*. Neptune City, New Jersey: TFH Publications. 240pp.

Basson, Philip W., Burchard, John E., Jr., Hardy, John T. & Price, Andrew R. G. (1977). *Biotopes of the Western Arabian Gulf*. Dhahran, Saudi Arabia: Aramco, Department of Loss Prevention and Environmental Affairs. 284pp.

Blegvad, H. (1944). *Danish Scientific Investigations in Iran*. Part III. Fishes of the Iranian Gulf. Copenhagen: Munksgaard. 247pp.

Breder, Charles M., Jr., & Rosen, Donn Eric (1966). Modes of Reproduction in Fishes. Garden City, New York: Natural History Press. 941pp. ·

Burgess, Warren & Axelrod, Herbert R. (1971–continuing). *Pacific Marine Fishes*. Vols I–VII. Hong Kong: TFH Publications.

Carcasson, R. H. (1977). *A Field Guide to the Coral Reef Fishes of the Indian and West Pacific Oceans*. London: Collins. 320pp.

Collette, Bruce B. (1974). The Garfishes (Hemirhamphidae) of Australia and New Zealand. *Records of the Australian Museum*, **39**(2): 11–105.

Eschmeyer, William N. & Rao, K. V. R. (1973). Two New Stonefishes (Pisces: Scorpaenidae) from the Indo-West Pacific, with Synopsis of the Subfamily Synanceiinae. *Proceedings of the California Academy of Science*, (Series 4) **39**(8): 337–382.

Kassler, P. (1973). The Structural and Geomorphic Evolution of the Persian Gulf. In: Purser, B. H. (Ed.), *The Persian Gulf*. New York: Springer-Verlag. Pp. 11–32.

Khalaf, K. T. (1961). *The Marine and Freshwater Fishes of Iraq*. Baghdad: Arbitta Press. 164pp.

Kuronuma, Katsuzo & Abe, Yoshitaka (1972). *Fishes of Kuwait*.

Kuwait: Kuwait Institute for Scientific Research. 123pp., 20 pl.

Lubbock, Roger (1975). Fishes of the Family Pseudochromidae (Perciformes) in the Northwest Indian Ocean and Red Sea. *Journal of Zoology, London*, **176**: 115–157.

Mahdi, N. (1971). Additions to the Marine Fish Fauna of Iraq. *Iraq Natural History Museum Publications*, **28**: 1–43.

Marshall, Tom C. (1965). *Fishes of the Great Barrier Reef and Coastal Waters of Queensland.* Narbaerth, Pennsylvania: Livingston. 566pp.

Menon, A. G. K. (1977). A Systematic Monograph of the Tongue Soles of the Genus *Cynoglossus.* Hamilton-Buchanan (Pisces: Cynoglossidae). *Smithsonian Contributions, Zoology*, **238**: 1–129.

Nadar, Iyad A. & Jawdat, Suad Z. (1977). New Records of Fishes from Iraq. *Bulletin Biological Research Center, Baghdad*, **8**, 73–87.

Nelson, Joseph S. (1976). *Fishes of the World.* New York: Wiley. 416pp.

Qureshi, M. R. & Bano, Anwari (1971). Common Gobioid Fishes of the Subfamilies Periophthalminae and Apocrypteinae. *Pakistan Journal of Science*, **23**(3–4): 143–146.

Regan, C. T. (1905). On Fishes from the Persian Gulf, the Sea of Oman and Karachi. Collected by Mr F. W. S. Townsend. *Journal of the Bombay Natural History Society*, **18**: 318–333.

Schultz, Leonard P. (1969). The Taxonomic Status of the Controversial Genera and Species of Parrot Fishes with a Descriptive List (Family Scaridae). *Smithsonian Contributions, Zoology*, **17**: 1–49, 8 pl.

Smith, J. L. B. (1965). *The Sea Fishes of Southern Africa* (5th Ed.). Capetown: Cape and Transvaal Printers. 580pp.

Smith-Vaniz, William F. (1976). The Saber-toothed Blennies, Tribe Nemophini (Pisces: Blenniidae). *Academy Natural Sciences of Philadelphia, Monograph 19*, 196pp.

Springer, Victor G. (1971). Revision of the Fish Genus *Ecsenius* (Blenniidae, Blenniinae, Salariini). *Smithsonian Contributions, Zoology*, **72**: 1–74.

Springer, Victor G. & Gomon, Martin F. (1975). Revision of the Blenniid Fish Genus *Omobranchus* with Descriptions of Three New Species and Notes on Other Species of the Tribe Omobranchini. *Smithsonian Contributions, Zoology*, **177**: 1–135.

136

Weber, M. & deBeaufort, L. F. (1936). *The Fishes of the Indo-Australian Archipelago*. Vol. 10, Leiden: E. J. Brill Ltd. 423pp.

White, A. W. & Barwani, M. A. (1971). *Common Sea Fishes of the Arabian Gulf and Gulf of Oman*. Trucial States Council, Dubai, Vol. I. 166pp.

Index of Scientific Names

138

139

140

145

Index of Common Names

147

148

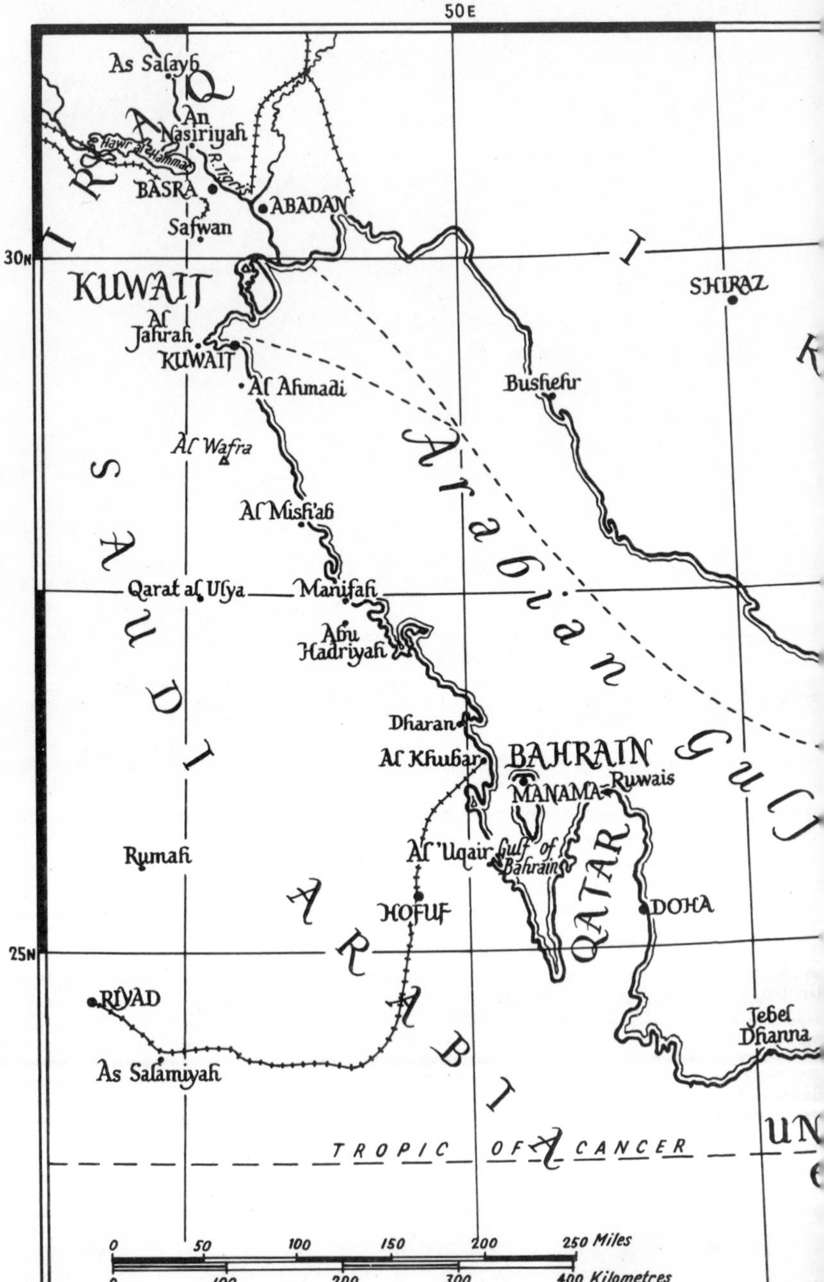
50E
As Salayb
IRAQ
An Nasiriyah
Hawr al Hammar
R. Tigris
BASRA
ABADAN
Safwan
30N
KUWAIT
Al Jahrah
KUWAIT
Al Ahmadi
Al Wafra
Al Mish'ab
Qarat al Ulya
Manifah
Abu Hadriyah
Dharan
Al Khubar
BAHRAIN
MANAMA
Ruwais
Al 'Uqair
Gulf of Bahrain
QATAR
DOHA
Rumah
HOFUF
25N
RIYAD
As Salamiyah
SAUDI ARABIA
Arabian Gulf
SHIRAZ
Bushehr
Jebel Dhanna
UN
TROPIC OF CANCER
0 50 100 150 200 250 Miles
0 100 200 300 400 Kilometres
50E